# Shifting Focus: A Handbook for ITV Educators

*Dianna Lawyer-Brook*
*Vicki McVey*

*illustrations by George Blevins*

The Scarecrow Press, Inc.
Technomic Books
Lanham, Maryland, and London
2000

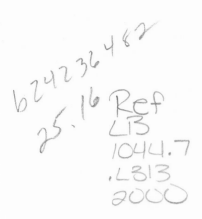
SCARECROW PRESS, INC.
Technomic Books

Published in the United States of America
by Scarecrow Press, Inc.
4720 Boston Way, Lanham, Maryland 20706
www.scarecrowpress.com

4 Pleydell Gardens, Folkestone
Kent CT20 2DN, England

British Library Cataloguing in Publication Information Available

**Library of Congress Cataloging-in-Publication Data**

Lawyer-Brook, Dianna, 1949–
    Shifting focus : a handbook for ITV educators / Dianna Lawyer-Brook and
    Vicki McVey.        p.    cm.
    Includes bibliographical references (p.  ) and index.
    ISBN 0-8108-3756-0 (alk. paper)
    1. Television in education—United States—Handbooks, manuals, etc.
    2. Interactive television—United States—Handbooks, manuals, etc.
    3. Teaching—United States—Aids and devices—Handbooks, manuals,
    etc. I. McVey, Vicki. II. Title.
    LB1044.7 .L313  2000
    371.33'58—dc21
                                                                    00-026696

∞™  The paper used in this publication meets the minimum requirements of American
National Standard for Information Sciences—Permanence of Paper for Printed Library
Materials, ANSI/NISO Z.39.48-1992.

# Contents

# Acknowledgments

We are very grateful to the following people for reading and commenting on the manuscript: Sally McVey, James F. Kettering, Carol Swinney, Phil Knight, and Jerry Walters. We would like to thank our family members for running errands, putting up with us, soothing our fevered brows, and fixing us medicinal beverages. You know who you are—we love you.

# 1

# Setting the Stage

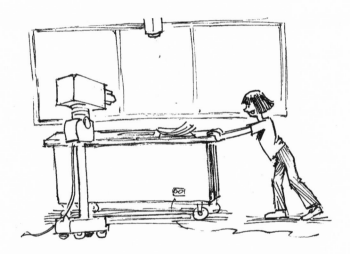

**QUESTIONS TO PONDER:**

1. Have you ever done something new, complicated, and totally unfamiliar without instruction or preparation?
2. Did it work, or did you wish you had practiced first?
3. Have you ever taught a class over two-way interactive television (ITV)?

Imagine a classroom without walls, but full of high-tech gadgets. Now imagine that everything you do in that classroom can be recorded by a video camera and saved for posterity. Scary, isn't it? If you are expanding your teaching repertoire to include two-way interactive television and are worried about finding yourself up to your knees in monitors and microphones without knowing how to use them, here are three things to think about:

- you aren't alone;
- "learning as you go" training is overrated; and
- this book is for you.

And if you aren't going to be teaching over the airwaves, but would like to add some interactive excitement and multimedia spice to your regular classroom recipe, this book is also for you.

  Glossary: For our purposes, **ITV** refers to two-way **I**nteractive **TeleV**ision—a video communications system that allows simultaneous, two-way audio and video connections across two or more sites.

## WHY THIS BOOK WAS WRITTEN

In many ways two-way interactive television (ITV) is an educator's dream. Our own experience has proved that it can open a world of possibilities for students in remote rural areas as well as inner-city neighborhoods; it can bring students from different parts of the world together into a single classroom and provide educational institutions with greatly expanded curricula. On the other hand, we have also seen these possibilities vanish as ITV systems were bought, put into use by untrained and intimidated staff, and sometimes left to gather dust after the first year of use.

With that in mind we have written this book for you, whoever you are. Whether you teach in the Goodacre Elementary School or Stanford University, you will find examples of ITV instruction that apply to your situation. As you might already have noticed, the style is informal rather than academic. We want to help you use this new technology, not think about it. Many of the examples we offer are from ITV classrooms or curricula that we have designed, written, or evaluated.

## WHAT THIS BOOK IS ABOUT

*Shifting Focus* takes three components of education and pulls them together in the context of distance learning:

- instructional content (the best content, aligned to standards);
- pedagogy (the most effective instructional strategies for use in the ITV environment); and
- technology (the best use of technology to deliver the content).

You will find *Shifting Focus* to be a practical guide to teaching over ITV. It uses a combination of research into the "state-of-the-art" of distance education, and the results of our many years of travel into the large, sometimes uncharted realm of educational interactive television. *Shifting Focus* is appropriate to any personal teaching style. If you're a forward-looking ham (like one of the coauthors) it will provide you with ideas, encouragement, and ways to double-check your progress. If you're shy but adventurous (like the other coauthor) it will give you clear and simple advice and activities, some tender loving care, and templates and forms. We have tried to base examples of ITV instruction on real-life situations in elementary, secondary, and postsecondary ITV classrooms.

## Overview of Chapters

Basically, the chapters of *Shifting Focus* follow the logical sequence you would use in preparing a class to be delivered over an interactive television system. Here is what you will find in this book.

Chapter 1, Setting the Stage—Besides explaining the mechanics of *Shifting Focus,* this chapter emphasizes the switch in thinking and teaching that will need to occur if you are to use the interactive television system to its full potential.

Chapter 2, Taking Care of Operational Issues—This chapter uses illustrations to help you get acquainted with the equipment you'll be working with in the ITV environment. It stresses the importance of working as a team player and using operational procedures to minimize students' perceptions of distance.

Chapter 3, What to Teach and How to Teach It—Chapter 3 shows you how to start at the ground floor by considering what types of pedagogy and instruction work best over interactive television. (Hint: it has to do with inquiring minds.) We also look at working with standards.

Chapter 4, Getting Ready—What do you need to do before the students arrive? How is your preparation different from that for your traditional classroom? What kind of lesson plan do you need? And what is that copyright thing about anyway?

Chapter 5, So Far and Yet So Near—This chapter includes a varied collection of practical strategies and activities, based on experience and research, that can be used in the classroom to decrease the feeling of distance. These strategies also support the planning done in the preceding chapters.

Chapter 6, Presentations with a Punch—How do you present all your wonderful ideas and materials in a manner that holds the students' attention? Interactive television has a wealth of possibilities for effective instruction through the use of multimedia tools, and this chapter will help you get to know some of them.

Chapter 7, Making Evaluation Work for You—How do you harness the evaluation beastie and turn it into one of the most helpful processes in your bag of tricks? Some reflection up front will save tears later. This chapter also contains essential information about structuring your class or program.

Chapter 8, That's What It's All About: Chapter Summaries—Definitely more detailed than these descriptions, but not onerous to read. Chapter 8 is a summary, a preview, or a reminder (depending on what you need).

Appendixes A and B—Appendix A provides some ideas for further reading; Appendix B has a fairly detailed self-assessment that follows the sequence of the chapters.

Glossary—Words that have been defined in each chapter are collected into a glossary at the end of the book.

## The Importance of Reflection

*Shifting Focus* will encourage you to shift your teaching approach by using "reflection." Although reflection might be one of the high-level thinking skills you have focused on in your classroom, this book will give you an opportunity to practice it. It will also provide information and activities to help you meet the needs of your students.

Important Point: Be sure to set aside time for reflection and practicing.

> **What Does It Look Like?**
>
> **Reflection**
>
> Do you save aluminum cans? Perhaps you are one of the many North Americans who spends time carefully sifting your garbage to help save the dwindling resources of our world. While conservation of our natural resources is important, there is another resource valuable to our personal and professional lives that teachers seldom take care of—spending time daily sifting through our minds and hearts, reflecting on how we can become more interesting and resourceful. Think of all the valuable ideas, hunches, insights, and feelings you will trash if you fail to become a reflective person and professional (Zehm and Kottler, 1993).

Glossary: **reflection**—reflection is the process of looking at our actions, decisions, or products, analyzing them by focusing on what we did or are doing, and learning lessons that can be applied to new situations.

The basic organization of this book will lead you through a process that includes reflection. Not only will practicing reflection help you model it for your students, but it will help you learn new concepts, adapt old procedures, and improve your teaching practices. At times you will be asked specific questions to consider, or you might be assigned tasks to be performed with peers. As a way of reinforcing your use of reflection, we recommend that you use a journal as you go through the book. Make a note to yourself to get a notebook, or relocate an old journal, to jot your ideas in as you read this book and implement your ITV classroom ideas.

## HOW TO USE THIS BOOK

*Shifting Focus* is designed so that, as you make your way through it, you will be creating interactive, multimedia ITV lessons. You will find that each chapter contains the same basic ingredients:

- Questions to Ponder (these questions will get you moving within the framework of the chapter);

- Glossary (new words, also found at the end of the book);

- Important Points (things not to miss);

- Caution (what not to do);

- Resources (references cited and suggested materials);

- Reflection (questions or suggestions to think about);

- Chapter Key Points (just what it sounds like); and

- Lights, Camera, Action (activities and exercises that will help you create your own ITV class).

## TECHNOLOGY AND TEACHING

No matter what your attitude is toward technology, electronic media have changed the way we view and deal with the world. Inside the classroom, technologies such as personal computers, e-mail, and the World Wide Web are revolutionizing both teaching and learning. The good news for teachers is that our use of technology is allowing us to redraw the map—stretching and sometimes even erasing boundaries between school, community, and the world. It is also providing opportunities that would not otherwise exist. The bad news is that if you don't know how to use electronic media you might spend some uncomfortable moments in front your class as you learn technologies that your students have already mastered.

 Reflection: Does using new technology intimidate you? Figure out whether it's a tool or a process that you're afraid of, and start a list.

One of the reasons we have written this book is to help you deal with the basic technology of interactive television before you have to use it. But technology is only one of the issues you'll be facing as you add ITV to your repertoire. Just as important is the psychological and pedagogical move from a classroom that is measured in square feet to one that is measured in square miles. To accomplish this move you will find yourself redefining your concept of the classroom and accepting the possibilities and challenges of using technology to create a new and potentially fascinating teaching and learning environment.

In making the move from the traditional to the ITV classroom, your teaching paradigm is probably going to undergo a major shift. You will have to find new ways to interact with your students. You will stretch yourself to come up with the multimedia materials that are so crucial to the ITV classroom, and you will discover that, while technology shapes the information it carries, *you* shape your use of the technology. We have designed *Shifting Focus* to help you do all these things.

New technology, when coupled with well-planned and supportive implementation, can facilitate radical change. For example, ITV is an ideal medium in which to experiment with moving away from lecture-oriented teaching methods toward more innovative techniques such as cooperative learning and authentic instruction. However, if teachers are not given the appropriate training and support to integrate these methods into their classrooms, they will likely resort to the methods with which they are most familiar and comfortable (Hobbs and Christianson, 1997).

So what's wrong with lecture-oriented teaching? Why won't it work over ITV?

Truthfully, nothing is wrong with lecture-oriented teaching over an ITV system, unless you have an objection to watching your students sleep through the entire class period. On the other hand, if snoozing students irritate you, you can shift your teaching paradigm, focus on learner-centered rather than content-centered instruction, and give everyone a break. In order to do this, however, your skills, delivery, and instructional techniques might have to change.

Reflection: Are you a risk-taker? If not, what kind of support can you pull together to help you make changes in your teaching style?

One of the greatest advantages of instruction over ITV is that it is often such a radical departure from traditional classroom teaching that it can kick a teacher right out of old, stale habits. The following is a true story.

Once upon a time a young Ph.D. was hired to help a medical school revamp its classroom instructional strategies. Although he was a specialist in instructional design, he was having a very difficult time prying these doctors out of their 55-minute lecture technique. He used various approaches, none of which was well received, to guide the doctors toward more interactive teaching methods.

But then the medical school started experimenting with distance learning. The doctors found themselves staring into video camera lenses, teaching to students at distant sites, and realizing that with interactive television, there is no "business as usual." Even worse, they suffered the mortification of watching their own heads on a television screen droning on, and on, and on. . . . Needless to say, our instructional specialist leapt into the fray and helped the doctors redesign their courses to include more interaction with their students.

Presto chango—the doctors moved toward a new teaching paradigm that not only worked in the ITV environment, but was transferred back into the traditional classroom to make the doctors more effective there, as well (Filipezak, 1996).

Reflection: Take the following self-quiz to find out how close your preconceptions about interactive television are to reality. Use your journal to jot down your reactions.

## *Exploding the Myth!*

1. If you know how to teach in a traditional classroom, you will know how to teach in an ITV classroom.          Yes _____          No _____
2. Students tend to be more frustrated by lack of interaction in an ITV classroom than in a traditional classroom.          Yes _____          No _____
3. Relationships and interaction are hard to maintain in an ITV classroom.
                                                          Yes _____          No _____
4. Since students watch TV, they will be comfortable "being on TV."
                                                          Yes _____          No _____
5. Planning a lesson for use over ITV doesn't take any longer than planning a traditional class.          Yes _____          No _____
6. If you're shy, being an ITV teacher will drive you crazy.
                                                          Yes _____          No _____
7. No matter how good it gets, teaching over interactive television can't be as effective as on-site, face-to-face instruction in the classroom.
                                                          Yes _____          No _____

(If you answered "yes" to any of the above questions, you need to adjust your attitude about educational interactive television.)

## THE WORLD OF DISTANCE LEARNING

According to the U.S. Congress, Office of Technology Assessment, "distance learning" is a viable and effective way of meeting educational needs in a time of educational reform. That sounds good, but where does ITV fit into distance learning?

Although the world of distance learning ranges from the fairly simple to the very complex (or from correspondence-based courses to telecommunications-based courses), at the high end it has almost as many gadgets as "Star Trek." Full-motion, two-way interactive television is the next best thing to being there. ITV technology can beam students at distant sites into the same virtual classroom, where they not only see and talk to each other, but can simultaneously take part in the same panel discussion.

Other video-based technologies offer lesser degrees of interaction. Although this book is specifically directed to a teacher working in the ITV environment, it is also "backward compatible" with other video-based delivery systems. In other words, teachers who find themselves working with one-way, video-based delivery systems (such as teleclasses or videocassettes), or with slow-motion TV or video-enhanced Internet communications, will also find plenty of help in *Shifting Focus*.

Reflection: Whether your school is elementary or college level, rural or urban, how can you best use ITV technology?

At its best, ITV takes the "lemon" of physical distance and can sweeten it into tasty lemonade that is enlivened by a diversity of students from different sites and backgrounds. At its best, ITV enhances student interaction rather than reducing it, and greatly expands limited course offerings, especially in small rural school districts, by offering things like:

- advanced high school courses;
- dual-credit college courses for high school seniors;
- course requirements for college admission;
- courses that require specialized teachers whose salaries can be shared among multiple school districts;
- special programs such as Title I, speech therapy, and so on.

At its worst . . . whew! At its worst, ITV is as passive and boring as the home-made video of your next-door neighbor's vacation. It reduces relationships among teachers and students to sterile interactions, and puts everyone to sleep. At its worst, ITV is a terrible mismatch between technology and education.

But worst-case scenarios can be avoided. In fact, there are many examples of teachers who have not only taught great classes over interactive television, but have even enjoyed it!

---

## Me? Replaced by a TV Set? Never!

### Carol J. Swinney, Hugoton High School, Hugoton, Kansas

Five years ago when my school district proudly announced that we were going to become a part of an interactive television network, my heart nearly stopped beating. After nearly twenty years in the traditional classroom, I felt a strange sensation deep in the pit of my stomach. . . . Yet after the initial shock wore off, I realized that the sensation growing in the depths of my body was not fear, but excitement.

Here was a chance to make the walls of my classroom invisible, to provide my students with experience in tomorrow's technology today, and to test the teaching skills I had developed so carefully for two decades.

Yet I stubbornly held on to the belief that techniques I had successfully used in the traditional classroom would translate to interactive television instruction. And I was right, sort of. I quickly learned that the elements of successful instruction were variety, visualization, and vigor. In fact, teaching interactive television has enlivened my traditional classroom as I have come to view my students, not as a captive audience, but as active participants in the process of communication and learning.

A final word of warning: It would be easy to become so enamored with the technology that one forgets the purpose of interactive television is to expand the learning opportunities of our students. Fiber optic technology is a valuable tool in the educational process, but it is not the teacher. In fact, in the successful ITV classroom, the technology is transparent.

So after five years as an interactive television instructor, the sensation of excitement still motivates me to explore new ways to use interactive television to educate my students. Me? Replaced by a TV? Never! But you can bet that I welcome the power of this technology to expand the world of learning for my students and me (Hobbs and Christianson, 1997).

In her ITV French classes Carol Swinney has done things like play "restaurant" with the waiter in one town and the customers in three others, and cook simultaneously in four locations. Her story points out one of the most interesting and entertaining aspects of teaching over two-way interactive television: it challenges your creativity, your ingenuity, and your ability to have fun.

Another example of effective use of ITV is a math class for elementary school students that was set up by the Northern Arizona University. The class was taught over ITV from a home site in Flagstaff to a remote site in Yuma. It focused on effective math practices, and was taught by a master teacher in Flagstaff. There were so many students attending at each site that several of the regular classroom teachers also attended the sessions. Although these teachers were there to support the instruction of their students, as the master teacher modeled the strategies, the classroom teachers practiced them with the students and at the same time learned effective instructional techniques. The experience turned out to be a highly effective form of staff development through modeling.

The final example of "best use" of ITV is presented to us from the students' perspective. The following quotes are from the journals of high school students who participated in a prototype experiment in international distance education. The class was called the "French Connection," and it brought students from rural Kansas and suburban Paris together to study current world geographic problems.

---

### Student Quotes from French Connection:

- It's awesome that someone so far away can feel like they are right in the room with you. It's exciting.
- The connections with France were astounding! To actually see and talk to teachers/students thousands of miles away was amazing.
- In my opinion, the second connect that dealt with neighborhood and surroundings was by far the best. During this connect the discussions centered around the towns where we lived, and what was located in and around those communities. In the case of the American side, many different towns of many different sizes were discussed while with the French, a city was discussed. I believe the French were most surprised about the amount of space around our towns, while we, the American students, were most impressed with the vastness of their city, Paris. In these ways we differed greatly, but in other ways, we had much in common. I believe this was the best connect because we were able to find out about each other, to find the differences in our cultures, but also to discover that we were very much alike.
- My favorite thing we learned about in this class was the GATT agreement [General Agreement on Tariffs and Trade]. It was very interesting for me to be able to research an issue and then debate it with the French students using the knowledge I gained during research. This type of education is very good for my type of person because it keeps my attention and allows me to be an active participant in it.

---

Important Point: Motivated students welcome the chance to participate. Believe it or not, the ITV classroom provides as many opportunities for student participation as the traditional classroom.

Caution: Don't underestimate the huge differences between traditional and ITV classrooms.

Given the fact that new instructional paradigms create an instant need for teacher training, it's surprising that this handbook hasn't been written earlier. (After all, if ITV is going to be used, it should be used to its greatest potential.) But unfortunately, innovations in educational technology are often so alluring that more technology is acquired than the training to go with it.

As you proceed through this book, keep in mind that technology is not magic. Its effectiveness depends on teacher training, expertise, and willingness to play and make a few mistakes. But even though the role of the teacher is pivotal, most ITV teachers begin with no experience on the system and little or no training.

> The critical role of the teacher in the distance learning setting makes it imperative that teachers get adequate training not only in the technical aspects of the system, but also in the educational applications of the technology.

—Congress of the United States, 1989

## CHAPTER 1 KEY POINTS

1. Electronic media are changing the way we see and deal with the world.
2. Learning anything that is as new, complicated, and demanding as teaching over two-way interactive television requires training and up-front practice.
3. Just as important as learning the new technology is making the psychological and pedagogical move from the traditional to the ITV classroom.
4. Lecture-oriented learning is a deadly bore over an ITV system.
5. If it is done right, two-way interactive television can take the "distance" out of distance education.
6. Technology is not magic. Its effectiveness depends on teacher training, expertise, and willingness to play and make a few mistakes.

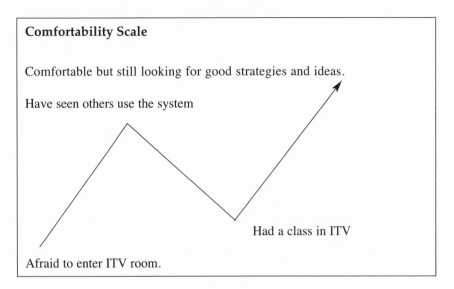

**Comfortability Scale**

Comfortable but still looking for good strategies and ideas.

Have seen others use the system

Had a class in ITV

Afraid to enter ITV room.

## LIGHTS, CAMERA, ACTION

1. Find the "Magic Matrix" (chapter 7, page 102), and use it to check in with yourself about the goals, objectives, and outcomes of your work. (This essential information is in the last substantive chapter because it is an integral part of the evaluation toolbox.)
2. Get a notebook or journal specifically for use with this book.
3. Ask a few friends and/or family members what they most hate about television; use your journal to number and write down each issue—don't forget to include your own.
4. Brainstorm ways that your ITV class could deal with each of the issues; number and write down your solutions to each one.

# 2

# Taking Care of Operational Issues

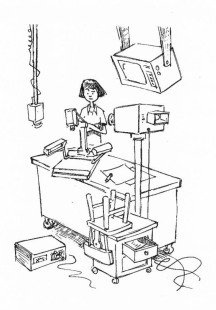

## QUESTIONS TO PONDER

1. Who is on your ITV team and what are their roles?
2. What needs to be planned besides the actual instruction?
3. What type of equipment configuration do you have and what does everything do?
4. How can you give additional support to students who are at a distant site?

## TEACHER AS TEAM PLAYER

Often, as an ITV teacher, you are solely responsible for the instruction of your students. But some districts or institutions of higher learning use site facilitators or technicians to support the teachers. Even luckier ITV teachers have access to support staff members including instructional designers, producers, graphic designers, photographers, and clerical assistants. Regardless of the number of staff, you alone, or you and your cohorts, must schedule opportunities to discuss upcoming lessons and how to improve the instruction. If other members of your team not only work at the remote sites, but live there too, time for conferencing should be scheduled over the ITV system before and/or after the transmission of the class.

Important Point: ITV teachers *must* have time scheduled for individual planning and planning with their team.

Caution: If you need time to meet with facilitators, technicians, or other teachers before or after your ITV class, be sure to schedule it in before the ITV schedules are firm. You might not be able to get the time after the schedules are set!

Glossary: **site facilitators**—teachers, paraprofessionals, parents, or other adults that facilitate the action at the distant ITV sites.

Glossary: **technicians**—the individuals who run the ITV system (if the job is not being done by the teacher).

Site facilitators are commonly found at remote sites. Not only do they come in different sizes and shapes (usually human shapes), they also vary in degree of expertise, experience, and responsibilities. We have seen experienced certified teachers fulfilling the role of facilitators at remote sites and assisting at the site where the head teacher was conducting the class. We have also seen parent volunteers in isolated regions who basically make sure the students are there and paying attention. The majority of site facilitators:

- make sure the equipment is on and running at the remote sites;
- distribute materials, assignments, and assessments;
- monitor discipline;
- fulfill liability requirements; and to varying degrees
- assist in instructional activities.

 Important Point: When working with younger children, the first responsibility of the site facilitator is to guarantee their safety—in other words, make sure that the students aren't bouncing off the walls.

Successful teaming with site facilitators depends not only on what each person brings into the relationship, but on the quality of the relationship as well. (Don't you wish that cooperative learning had been required for our generation?) Regardless of the facilitator's role, it is imperative that there be constructive, cooperative, and respectful teaming among the staff. If it sounds like we're making this up, try working with a facilitator or a technician who has a conflict of interest and is capable of sabotaging you—not a pretty picture.

The selection of the site facilitators might be beyond the teacher's control, but the teacher can still promote good teaming and successful instruction by:

- engaging the facilitators immediately in the beginning of the planning process as well as working with them throughout the year;
- providing copies of all outlines, lesson plans, slides, etc. to the facilitators in advance;
- making sure there is a common understanding of everyone's responsibilities;
- modeling effective interactions with students; and
- encouraging ongoing feedback and discussions on improvement.

The best site facilitators mimic the best teachers in their enthusiasm and ability to provide support to the instruction, monitor the students' level of engagement, answer questions, be ready with materials and supplies, and provide ongoing feedback to the teacher. In addition to all that, they are whizzes with the equipment.

 Caution: Regardless of how overwhelmed or distracted you get, be sure to maintain good relationships with your facilitators or other team members. Relationships among the staff determine the mood for the class.

 Reflection: When considering all the facets of an ITV program and your own strengths/weaknesses, what type of personality and skills should *your* team have?

In addition to brainstorming and feedback from the facilitators, all ITV teachers need peer support and ideas from other teachers using the ITV. If there is only one ITV teacher at the site, it is especially important that the teacher has access to e-mail, the Internet, downlinks, and professional conferences for outside input and support.

Important Point: ITV teachers need opportunities to interact with other ITV teachers.

## TEACHER AS MANAGER

Teaching over the ITV delivery system takes a lot of concentration, even when everything runs smoothly. So it is essential that every element be well planned and structured to eliminate problems. To support this seamless delivery of instruction, some basic administrative components and operational issues need to be addressed. These components include paying attention to staff development, scheduling, discipline, budgets, emergencies, equipment, and additional support to distant sites.

### Staff Development

Sadly, there are several staff development problems that commonly occur with new ITV programs:

- Staff development might be entirely overlooked.
- If there is training, it might focus on how to use the equipment rather than how to teach over the system.
- Even when teachers are trained on the ITV system, it is possible that those with training might leave, and no one else is trained to carry on.

Everyone connected with the ITV program should have *some* elementary understanding of the system—how it works and how to make it work well. This includes the administrators, other designated teachers in the building, support staff, potential substitutes, and if suitable, parents. *At least* one month before classes begin, the new ITV teacher should have training on the system and learn how to fully utilize it for instruction. A full month is necessary for the teacher to design lessons and to practice using the system. This step is crucial both for the peace of mind of the teacher and for the quality of instruction. You can't disguise lack of preparedness. Looking like a fool in front of your class is bad enough, but having it broadcast and recorded for posterity is far worse.

Reflection: Sometimes extensive practicing is more important for peace of mind than for anchoring skills. Sometimes we have the skills, but nervousness gets in the way. Are you this type of person or is nervousness not a factor?

## Scheduling

Scheduling is another important detail that needs to be taken care of early in the planning phase. Even under the simplest of circumstances (in other words, where ITV isn't involved) scheduling classes is so complicated that high schools and colleges dedicate personnel only for that purpose. When you bring ITV into the picture, aligning a number of schools or sites to share classes over the system can be a nightmare—and will be if it isn't done in advance. Various building sites might have different holidays and scheduling requirements (for example, traditional versus block scheduling), and it can be downright painful to adjust class times. Also, remember time zone differences between designated sites. We had an international program that had a seven-hour time difference, so that one site started class at 6 or 7 a.m. (depending on daylight savings time), and the other site started at 2 p.m.

Caution: Be sure that the schedule is solidified well in advance of the ITV classes.

## Discipline

Discipline is a key factor in the ITV classroom, as it is in any other. But the ITV situation is also unique. One thing that can aid discipline is to create a contract that can be signed by students and their parents, stating that attending an ITV class is a privilege that can be revoked at any time. (Most students really do see it that way and are excited about attending the ITV classes.) Another important boost to discipline (especially in K-12 education) is the presence of an adult or facilitator at the remote sites. One tiny rural district had the office secretary observe the classroom from across the hall while answering phones and performing other duties.

---

### Sample Student Contract

I understand that participating in this class and using ITV equipment is a privilege that can be revoked at any time. I therefore agree to the following:

1. I assume responsibility for my own learning. This means that I will be present, attentive, participatory, and will complete all assignments.
2. I won't use inappropriate language or gestures.
3. I won't use any piece of equipment unless directed by a teacher or paraprofessional.
4. I will not damage or deface the facility or any equipment in it.
5. I know I can be videotaped at any time.
6. This contract specifically addresses conduct in the ITV classroom; I will still adhere to general policies for student conduct as recognized by my home school.

_____     _____     _____
Student signature          Parent signature           Teacher signature

---

Reflection: What would be the most important statements to have in your student contract?

## Budget

Having a budget that includes resources beyond the normal allotment is not only beneficial to the program, but it also motivates the teacher. ITV instruction is resource hungry, both in materials and staff time to be set aside for design and implementation. Since commercial materials are not designed for use over ITV, you must either create or adapt your own. If you are adapting commercial materials, you might have to negotiate and pay for copyright permission (even if you only plan to use short selections), and this can be costly both in time and money. So if at all possible, extra money needs to be budgeted for teacher time, materials, copyright permissions, and other related expenses.

Important Point: Money (or additional resources) makes the world (ITV) go around (or at least go around better).

## Emergencies

In 1994, we conducted a pilot project that used ITV to link a number of rural school districts in southwest Kansas with schools in a cosmopolitan suburb of Paris. The students from each country came together in a linked classroom to study and analyze global issues. The highlight of the project was a series of international hook-ups broadcast, on the U.S. side, from different participating Kansas schools. Teachers' journals were used as part of the formal project evaluation, and the following story is based on one of the Kansas teachers account of the day she hosted her first international "hook-up." Because of the difference in time zones, the class in Kansas was scheduled at 6 a.m.

> The year of the pilot project was also this teacher's first year using the interactive television system. She awoke very early on a snowy morning—it was the day her school was to host the international hook-up—to get everything ready. All week the students had discussed the upcoming hook-up with France, and had been preparing for the visiting local districts as well as the connection with the Parisian students. Everyone was very excited.
>
> After getting ready and closing the door, she rushed to her car and realized too late that the car keys were not only locked in the house, but were on the same ring as the house and the ITV classroom keys. She ran through the snow to the school and brought the custodian back to climb to the second story of her house, where the windows were not locked. He then proceeded to open her front door. She grabbed the keys, jumped in the car, rushed to the school, opened her room, let the guests in, and switched on the monitors. Just at that moment, the connection was completed and the Parisian students came on the monitor.

No matter how prepared you are, "stuff happens." However, to what degree the "stuff" interrupts your instruction often depends on how prepared you are. "Happening stuff" includes:

- accidental cutting of the cable;
- lightning strikes;
- power failure;
- snow days, asbestos removal, broken pipes (can't do anything about it);
- an absent teacher (might be able to do something about it); or
- equipment not functioning (can do something about it).

So we won't discuss the first type of emergencies except to suggest praying that the snow, asbestos, or water does not get into the equipment. If you are the missing teacher, here are some ways you can prepare for your absence.

*How to prepare for absent teachers:*

- Train substitutes with teachers
- Identify substitutes who like ITV

- Invite substitutes to visit ahead of time
- Have additional lessons taped
- Have lesson plans ready ahead of time
- Provide a "substitute or guest" book that lists procedures, settings, and phone numbers

The last group of emergencies—equipment not functioning—will be discussed in the next section.

## BECOMING ONE WITH YOUR EQUIPMENT—OR "IT'S ALIVE!!!"

Probably the most intimidating aspect of teaching over an ITV system is the equipment. As a general rule, most teachers have not had much experience with video equipment except for programming VCRs and running hand-held video cameras. Because of this lack of expertise, it is important for you to familiarize yourself with the equipment and classroom before classes actually begin.

Important Point: Do not use equipment you haven't been properly introduced to. Introductions and a courting period are a must.

What does an ITV classroom look like? ITV classroom composition varies from the bare minimum set-up, to the complex "ready for commercial broadcasting" studio. We have seen a number of successful programs using set-ups from both ends of the spectrum. Each type of ITV classroom composition has advantages and disadvantages for the teacher.

Teacher Controlled Set-up: A very low cost version used by many rural school districts (see illustration on p. 23) contains three cameras, six to eight monitors, a teacher desk, student desks, and microphones in a windowless classroom (natural lighting can interfere with the cameras). One camera is focused on the teacher standing behind the desk, another focuses on the group of students, and a third is mounted above and focuses downward onto top of the teacher's desk. Three of the monitors are in front of, to the side of, or over the teacher's desk, so that the students in the classroom can see the other sites. The other three monitors are behind and above, or to the side of the students so that the teacher can see their images at all sites simultaneously. Student microphones are either on the ceiling, free standing, or on the students' desks. The teacher's microphone is generally attached to her clothes or mounted above her desk.

Control of the three cameras rests in the hands of the teacher. Not only can she choose what camera is in use, but she can also control the direction and degree of magnification. Pushing one of three buttons initiates camera selection; zooming, panning, and tilting are accomplished by using the appropriate toggle switch.

Glossary: **zooming**—movement of the camera lens forward or backward, causing the item that is being viewed to appear larger or smaller.

 Glossary: **panning**—moving the camera side-to-side across the room.

 Glossary: **tilting**—moving the camera up or down.

The teacher is in charge of the video production. She has full control of what is viewed by the students. There is no technician to direct the camera for her and, by the same token, no technician with whom she has to coordinate. But, as we tell students, with power comes responsibility. The teacher must be aware at all times of where the camera is directed, as well as teach her lesson.

 Caution: Do not leave the camera pointing towards empty space during instruction. Blank screens get boring.

Technician Controlled Set-up: The main difference between this classroom and the one above is that this one has a small control room which contains a videotape machine, remote controls, an audio board, and a console for monitoring cameras. A technical assistant is required to do the camera work. The teacher does not manage the cameras and related equipment—that is the job of the technician. The advantage of this set-up is that the teacher can focus on teaching and let the technician worry about where the camera is. Generally, this expensive set-up has more snazzy equipment, such as the character generators that will be discussed later. The final presentations will probably be more sophisticated than when the teacher does it alone. Because of the additional human and technical factors, pre-planning and following a detailed outline is essential and this coordination takes more time. Another disadvantage to this complex set-up is the loss of on the spot flexibility.

*Specific Equipment Found in the ITV Classroom*

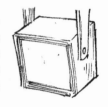

Monitors are larger versions of the screens we use with computers and televisions. Students from remote sites can see the teacher on a monitor. Students can see their classmates from the other sites on the monitors. The teacher can see the students in her room and at the distant sites. Sometimes the screen of a monitor is divided so that each site is visible to the teacher and all the students (split mode). This works well on a large monitor, but some school districts have more than four sites and so rotate the image of the different sites after specific intervals (scan mode). For many people this rotation is distracting and makes in-depth interaction difficult.

 Glossary: **split mode**—division of the monitor into quadrants, one for each site.

 Glossary: **scan mode**—periodic rotation of images on the monitor, from one site to another.

 Caution: To have the highest amount of interaction, you need to be able to see the students continuously. Be sure your system allows this visual connection.

Often the ITV teacher's favorite piece of equipment is the overhead (also called graphic or document) camera. The camera has many names, sometimes even being called by its brand name, "Elmo." The overhead camera has a variety

## What Does It Look Like?

Students at the home site are watching their teacher demonstrate how the Huns spread across Europe on a map shown through the use of the overhead camera. She stimulates discussion by asking questions about map elements. The students can also see their classmates at the three remote sites answering questions when called upon. This is done through the use of a very large monitor next to the teacher that is split into four quadrants, with a view of each site. The map can be seen in fourth quadrant. The teacher can choose to make the large monitor only show the map.

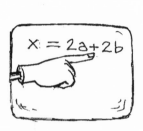

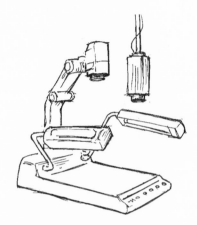

of functions. As mentioned in the previous section, this camera points down at the desk and can take the place of a chalkboard. In addition, because the camera can zoom, small objects can be seen with greater clarity than with the naked eye across the room. Some new Elmos are able to rotate around an object, providing a three-dimensional view of it. Transparencies can be viewed with a piece of plain paper behind them or slides can be shown with a light box behind them.

Caution: All images will be shown in a three-by-four-ratio. You need to plan for this shape. Taping a paper frame at this ratio under the overhead camera helps remind you and gives guidelines for object placement.

Glossary: **four-by-three ratio**—the formula that describes the relationship between the height and the width of a graphic designed for a TV monitor. We are accustomed to pages that are taller than they are wide (portrait mode)—a camera sees and projects in a "landscape" mode, which is wider than it is tall.

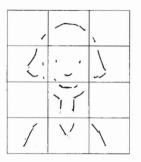

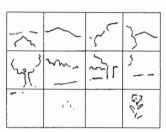

**Portrait Mode**                    **Landscape Mode**

## What Does It Look Like?

When teaching a segment on the history of education, Professor Dave Harmon amassed a collection of photographs of school buildings. Many of these were photos from the 1800s, including one-room schoolhouses. As he talked, he flipped the images on the "Elmo" every five to ten seconds. He didn't necessarily comment on the photos, but used them to draw the students into his lecture and constantly change the pace.

Professor Harmon teaches over two-way interactive video at the multicampus Colorado Mountain College. He says that "It is especially important to plan fast-paced presentations when using the Elmo. This sounds like a lot of trouble, but it really isn't. Just keep in the habit of constantly thinking about materials you can use, and things will present themselves to you readily."

## What Does It Look Like?

The teacher is doing a lesson on making change. As she gives her example, she places the correct coins under the overhead camera and zooms the camera to show the markings clearly both for the third graders in the sending classroom and the receiving sites. The students can see the differences more clearly than if she was trying to hold the coins up in front of the traditional classroom.

The character generator is a computer that can be set to display short messages across the video screen. These messages can include key words or concepts such as definitions, quotes, instructions, topical headings, and homework. When you see phrases across your television screen on the evening news, the production station is using a character generator.

Glossary: **character generator**—a special computer that generates short messages and displays them on top of the image on the monitor.

Caution: The sizing rules that pertain to overhead transparencies also apply to the computer-generated lettering. Watch the size and type of the font and the length of the message.

---

### What Does It Look Like?

The students are starting to study a new theme from geography. As the teacher begins her discussion, the title of the geographic theme, "Relationships between People and Places," appears at the bottom of the video screen.

---

Microphones are a requirement for audio transmission, so some type of microphone will be found in every ITV classroom. Microphones have the capability of driving instructors insane. Many microphones are hung from the ceiling or built into the desks/tables, but some are freestanding on the desks in front of the students. This allows for the amplification of pencil drum rolls on the tables. Even minimum handling by the students can be distracting.

Caution: Misuse of microphones can be distracting or even painful. Discover what type of system you have and plan accordingly.

Important Point: Establish guidelines in the beginning that define appropriate behavior with the microphones. Remind students not to rustle papers, have side conversations, place books in front of the microphones, or speak away from the microphones.

---

### What Does It Look Like?

The students in a classroom in Minnesota must push the button on their microphone to speak to the teacher and to be heard by the other sites. In the beginning of the classes, students often forget to push the buttons, which usually gets an immediate reaction from the other sites.

---

FAX machines can quickly scan and send documents over the telephone wires to the remote sites. The tool is very helpful to the ITV instructor, cutting down on travel time and making memo delivery almost immediate. The FAX can be used for assignments and assessments, but print quality varies depending on the machine.

Important Point: For FAX machines: Write only on one side, use black or red ink (no blue ink or pencil), leave a margin, avoid using paper that has ragged edges, and number your pages.

Caution: Depending on the FAX machines for last minute assessments can be a mistake. FAX machines can jam or otherwise get held up. Plan in advance and deliver copies early to your distant sites.

---

**What Does It Look Like?**

The ITV teacher found an article in the morning paper that discussed a plane crash that was related to an aerodynamics formula that the class would be discussing later in the week. She faxed the article to the facilitators at each site, to be used as an additional reading assignment for class discussion.

---

There is a reason for the amazing proliferation of videocassette recorders (VCRs) in schools. The VCR can be used for many purposes, including playing short video clips to generate interest in the subject, recording entire lessons for absent students, preparing lessons ahead of time when the teacher will be absent, and videotaping the class in session. Many VCRs also have a video-recording switch, which allows the teacher to record from any camera in the system (including those at the remote sites). In evaluating a joint international ITV class, the researchers used tapes of the classes to get a feel for the classes and students' reactions.

Caution: Using commercial videotapes might infringe on copyright laws. Read the section on copyright in chapter 3 and be familiar with the local interpretations.

---

**What Does It Look Like?**

One of the students in the ITV classroom was going to miss the next class session, because he had a parent getting married out of state. Apparently, the parent felt that the student should be there. As the teacher made it a habit to tape each session, it was relatively easy to set up a time that the student could view the missed class. The student had suggested taping the wedding instead, but the parent did not approve that idea.

---

Some classrooms have computers with CD-ROM players linked directly into the system so that they can use the capacity of the computer for broadcasting. This equipment supports the addition of simulation and presentation software that can be directly shown over the system.

Caution: Always run any type of software ahead of time to make sure it will function in the way you desire.

## What Does It Look Like?

During a lesson on table and chart making, the teacher runs an example from National Geographic's "Project Zoo." This software demonstrates how the bars in bar graphs represent values. The snakes that are measured in the program actually become the bars, through the magic of the computer.

What if you have all this wonderful equipment and it doesn't work? Sometimes various components of an ITV classroom don't "work" especially in the beginning. What do you do when this happens?

Important Point: Try to take deep breaths and not panic when equipment is not working. And remember, generally you can't break the equipment unless you are physically forcing pieces into wrong places.

The following troubleshooting procedure is based on a list in Hobbs and Christianson's *Virtual Classrooms: Educational Opportunity through Two-Way Interactive Television,* an excellent resource book.

## Basic Guidelines for Troubleshooting ITV Problems

1. Don't panic. Try turning everything off and then on again.
2. Check all switches:

   - Is the switch off or on?
   - Is the volume turned up?
   - Are the batteries dead?

3. Check all settings. Are they correct? (This takes some preplanning—do you know what they are supposed to be?)
4. Work forward and backward to narrow the problem.
5. Get help from someone who knows.
6. Have a backup plan. Use what you have working, namely the video or audio to give an assignment.
7. Get it on tape if possible.
8. Record all problems and solutions in a written log.

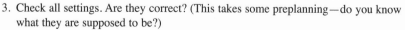

Equipment not working is a major complaint from teachers with new ITV systems. A good idea would be to give the staff that assembles the equipment plenty of time and trials to get rid of all the bugs.

## SUPPORT AT A DISTANCE

If most of your students are miles away from where you live and work, how do you provide an environment that supports their learning? How can you provide mentoring for someone that you might never even shake hands with? This is a concern that beginning ITV teachers often voice.

The good news is that there are a number of operational strategies that can be used to decrease the feelings of distance and isolation. The next two chapters will detail some instructional strategies that aim to minimize distance, but luckily for us there are also standard operational procedures that support learning at a distance. These procedures include using study groups, emphasizing links with the facilitators, responding quickly to student needs, getting materials to them promptly, providing interactive study guides, incorporating community resources, and using the Internet.

The human element is crucial in decreasing distance, even when considering structure and operational procedures. The teacher or facilitators should encourage or even preorganize study groups among the students at the sites. As mentioned earlier, the role of being a bridge and a link to the students should be stressed to the facilitators.

Important Point: Remote study groups reinforce learning, promote peer collaboration, and increase face to face contact.

The immediate handling of questions, assignments, and tests is a reflection of the quality of support and consideration that the teacher has for students at the distant sites. A procedure must be in place for students to have their questions answered either in class or after class by e-mail/telephone. A quick response time is crucial. The same is true for assignments and tests. Turnaround time needs to be short, and comments make more impact when they are personalized or individualized. The equipment discussed earlier, such as the fax machine and computers, supports quick responses. Telephones can also be used to answer questions, but many find the e-mail easier with everyone's busy schedule. The teacher needs to be seen as being easily accessible.

Glossary: **e-mail**—electronic mail—messages sent and received via a computer and telephone lines.

Important Point: Feedback in all forms must be immediate.

Timely delivery of materials to the remote sites also makes a statement about the teacher's or school's support to the student. No one likes to be participating in a class without the right materials. A system needs to be developed that guarantees delivery of class materials or tests before they are needed. Faxes can be used as backup.

Important Point: Make sure class materials and assessments are delivered on time.

One way of helping students organize their own work is to create an Interactive Study Guide that you will distribute before the class begins. This study guide is a highly organized set of student notes, graphics, and activities to be used in conjunction with your ITV class. Providing them with notes allows students to process information rather than copying it down during class, and it also helps them prioritize concepts according to what is "noteworthy" and what isn't. The study guide can be made interactive by leaving out important concepts and terms and providing space for students to write them in (Cyrs and Smith, 1990).

There are a number of community resources that can support ITV instruction. Libraries at remote sites, academic and public, can make video and written materials available for students taking ITV classes. Collaborating with local schools and community centers can often provide additional resources for your students. Schools, libraries, and community centers might also have links to the Internet that can be utilized to enhance instruction.

Important Point: Look into what is available for your students at their sites.

*Why do you want to use the Internet to support your ITV instruction?*

- Current and historical information is immediately accessible on the World Wide Web;
- Students can express their ideas in chat rooms and through sharing assignments over a list serv;

- Students can get outside expert perspectives through e-mail;
- Students can develop peer relationships;
- Using the Internet is a life-long valuable skill; and
- It is fun.

Glossary: **list serv**—a list of e-mail users who can send messages to all other members on the list simultaneously

Important Point: Be sure to take advantage of any Internet possibilities with your students.

Appendix A has a list of good books for teachers on the use of the Internet.

## CHAPTER 2 KEY POINTS

1. Often the ITV instructor will be working with a number of support personnel.
2. This team should have ample time to plan and improve the program.
3. The site facilitators' roles might vary, but they are crucial to the success of the instruction and should be involved in planning from the beginning.
4. Planning, introductory training, setting schedules, discipline, and incorporating resources all need to be addressed before classes begin.
5. Plans made ahead of time addressing the unexpected (absent teacher, etc.) make life easier.
6. Equipment can be your friend if time is taken to become acquainted with its function and settings.
7. Equipment typically found in an ITV room includes monitors, graphic cameras, character generators, microphones, fax machines, VCRs, and computers.
8. A logical plan can be followed to troubleshoot equipment problems.
9. Ways of creating a supportive learning environment at a distance include the effective use of facilitators, study groups, and the Internet. Having frequent and immediate feedback also promotes engagement and learning.
10. Possible sources of assistance and materials might include academic and public libraries, other schools, and community centers at the remote sites.

## LIGHTS, CAMERA, ACTION

1. Visit the camera room where you will be transmitting your classes and make yourself familiar with all of the equipment. You might need a technician or director to help you understand the various technologies and plan for contingencies.
2. Visit the remote sites.
3. Create an equipment notebook for yourself and future substitutes that describes the equipment, its function, settings, and what can go wrong and how to fix it.
4. Make sure your team is in agreement about roles and responsibilities. Take your lesson plan from the previous chapter and consider how your team could work together on completing it successfully. How would each team member add to the whole? (that is, what would the facilitators do, etc.?)
5. Make contingency plans that will cover your absence, a student's absence, a snow day at one of the sites, or an equipment shutdown.

## 3

# What to Teach and How to Teach It

**QUESTIONS TO PONDER:**

1. If the teaching model you use works in a traditional class-room, will it work in the ITV environment?
2. How can you approach "the same old stuff" in a new way for interactive television?

For thousands of years people have used audio or visual technology to communicate with each other simultaneously over distance. Audio technology included stuff like drums, conch shells, and animal horns, and people with extremely loud voices in high towers. Visual technology rested on other things like smoky fires and wet blankets, sun and mirrors, and pieces of bright-colored cloth hung from tall poles. As inventive and effective as their technologies were, our ancestors left it up to us to discover electricity, combine the audio with the visual, and create television. But even this crowning achievement was limited by the fact that it was one-way. In fact, interaction with a television is so passive that a new term "couch potato," had to be invented to describe the TV viewer.

Luckily, new developments in television broadcasting are moving us out of the couch potato phase and into possibilities for instantaneous interactive communication via television. But, as you might guess from its name, two-way interactive television doesn't work unless interaction is taking place. Because this is so, the pedagogy that has evolved around educational two-way interactive television has a tremendous focus on interaction. And guess whose job it is to make interaction happen?

- Other teachers?
- The Superintendent?
- The School Board?
- Congress?
- You?

One of the "Questions to Ponder" above asks whether or not the teaching model you use in your traditional classroom will work in the ITV environment. Well, the answer to that depends on how successful you are at promoting interaction among your students, and how good you are at creating a classroom where they also interact with learning materials to construct their own genuine (and probably idiosyncratic) understanding. Depending on these things, your current teaching paradigm might need a little modification here and there, or you might need to adopt an entirely new paradigm. We've included the following self-test to help you assess your need to modify or change the learning model you are using.

     Reflection: Teaching Style Self-Test

- How often do you use worksheets (elementary level) or lectures (secondary and postsecondary levels) to convey information to your students?
- Are you more likely to hand out information, or to have students find it for themselves?
- Are the kids interacting with each other and you, or do they spend more time reading, listening, and/or working by themselves?
- In a discussion, are you more likely to facilitate or direct?
- Are you more likely to answer questions, or to ask them?

- Is most of your assessment of the students based on written tests, or is it performance-based?
- Do you base your teaching on resources readily available, or do you search for and/or invent your own resources to match your students' learning styles?

Caution: If your teaching style doesn't constantly promote interaction and exploration, it won't work on ITV.

Some of the techniques that you've used successfully in the traditional classroom can be disastrous over the ITV system. Probably the best example (or at least the most notorious) of these is the dreaded "talking head" syndrome. In its less deadly manifestation this technique is known as the common lecture. It sounds innocent enough, but if you want to experience severe to life-threatening boredom, go find a segment from one of the earliest educational TV programs. You will see a television screen filled with the torso and head of someone who, were it not for the moving lips, would be about as lively as a plaster bust of Beethoven.

## THE CONSTRUCTIVIST THEORY

The good news is that there are a few learning models that can be transferred very effectively to the ITV environment. For instance, according to both the research and our own experience in the field, teaching strategies based on the constructivist theory make for very effective instruction over ITV.

Glossary: **constructivist theory**—the idea that learning involves a student's direct interaction with the subject matter, and that understanding comes out of that interaction. The teacher is a facilitator of this process.

The constructivist theory rests on the idea that effective learning takes place when a student interacts with learning materials, constructing out of this interaction her own unique understanding and internal representation of knowledge. According to Kemp and Smellie, constructivism is based on the following assumptions:

- knowledge is constructed from experience;
- learning is an active process, with experience leading to meaning;

- learning should occur in realistic settings;
- growth in understanding concepts comes from experiencing many perspectives relative to a situation, then adjusting beliefs in response to new perspectives; and
- testing should be integrated with the task, not treated as a separate activity.

(Kemp and Smellie, in Hobbs and Christianson, 1997)

Within this paradigm, learning becomes a process of knowledge building that engages the teacher and students. It doesn't matter what the subject matter is, only that the students interact with the materials to create their own experience of learning. Instead of lecturing the students, the teacher facilitates and participates in this exploration, discovery, and learning.

Important Point: Expand the materials and the discussion to show your students more than one perspective.

A woman named Barbara Means created a handy list of seven constructivist-type variables that indicate whether or not effective teaching and learning are taking place. These variables stress the interactivity and involvement of the students, and therefore can be borrowed in their entirety and used to diagnose effective teaching and learning in the ITV environment.

- The teacher is a facilitator in learning.
- Students learn through exploration.
- Students are engaged in authentic and multidisciplinary tasks.
- Students participate in interactive modes of instruction.
- Students work collaboratively.
- Students are grouped heterogeneously.
- Assessments are based on students' performance of real tasks.

(Jones, et al., 1995)

As a facilitator your job is to orchestrate inquiry (which is covered in the following section), to coordinate materials and technology, and to facilitate personal interactions among the students and between the students and you. Rather than acting the role of "voice of authority" in your classroom, you will be exploring, with your students, various academic realms.

 Important Point: Remember that you aren't just working with a new instructional paradigm, but adapting your teaching style to a medium that has tremendous multimedia possibilities.

Two-way interactive television will allow you to do things with learning materials that you might never have dreamed of. You can (and should) use this technology for all it's worth; it will allow you to bring all sorts of dynamic elements into your lessons.

For instance, we know that students have various ways of learning, so it makes sense that they will respond to different stimuli. With the multimedia possibilities of ITV you can use various media (for example, print, slides, videotapes) and interactive techniques (for example, debates, simulations, role playing) to "play to the strengths" of all of your students, no matter what their learning styles are. And by the way, if creating multimedia lessons and engineering interactive activities in several classrooms simultaneously sounds overwhelming, that's why you're using this book. The quote from Carol J. Swinney in chapter 1 (page 10) is ample proof that a total neophyte can do a great job.

 Important Point: Remember that your students have different learning styles—don't expect them all to respond to the same things.

In addition, as you switch your role from "presenter" to "facilitator," there are several characteristics of good instruction that you can incorporate into your les-

sons. Using the following list will improve your teaching in general, and will help
guarantee your effectiveness over ITV.

Effective instruction is:

- Experiential (leading the students into an experience of what the lesson is
  about).
- Relevant (with obvious connections to things that are real in the students'
  lives).
- Active (engaging the participation of the students).
- Complex (leading the students to think rather than memorize).
- Knowledge building (creating and/or building on links with other things the
  students have learned or are interested in).
- Authentic (coming from and creating real experiences and processes).

## THE INQUIRY APPROACH

Inquiry-based instruction is another of the teaching approaches that transfers
seamlessly into the ITV environment (and therefore has a lot in common with the
constructivist theory). In general, the inquiry model puts the student and the
teacher into the roles of data gatherer and analyst, while maintaining the teacher's
position as organizer and facilitator. In other words, instead of delivering a prefabricated body of knowledge, the teacher facilitates (and engages in) a process
of investigation and analysis with his students.

 Reflection: When using the inquiry approach over the system
you can turn the physical distance between sites to your advantage. Think of appropriate local investigations that will allow
students at the different sites to come up with their own data
(for example, looking at election results, soil types, etc., from
the different communities).

Because there isn't a pre-existing body of knowledge to base the investigation
on, students develop critical thinking skills as they inquire, gather and analyze
data, and reach conclusions. Although each student engages in her own unique
learning process, she also brings her experience into the group, helping to create
a learning community with a shared knowledge base. As students develop critical thinking skills, they also establish a cognitive link between "academic" and
"practical" knowledge.

### Key Distinctions Between Inquiry and Traditional Lecture Approaches

Issue-based inquiry takes the inquiry model a step further, defining a preselected
real-world issue or problem, and then focusing an investigation on its possible

| | |
|---|---|
| Students examine data as evidence and draw conclusions | Students are presented information in a lecture or textbook |
| Learning environment supports ambiguity and encourages questions | Learning environment supports "right answers" |
| Students continuously create knowledge base, so problems have multiple solutions | Knowledge base is prefabricated, problems have single, already identified solutions |
| Students talk, write, and collaborate as means of clarifying concepts/ideas | Concepts/ideas are clarified by the teacher or textbook |
| Students acquire cognitive skills in the process of investigating, analyzing, drawing conclusions | Students are given information that leads them to memorize rather than think |

solution(s). Whether the class is math, literature, or geography, this approach creates a link between academic knowledge and the ability to understand and analyze what is happening in the world outside of school. Because real-world case studies can be selected for relevance to students' lives, such case studies often engage the students' interest and interaction where hypothetical situations might not.

 Caution: Real-world issues might be even more interesting to the teacher than to the students . . . if you choose an extremely "hot" topic, be prepared to put out the fires.

Real-world case studies also promote a high degree of interaction among the students. And because of the dynamic and social nature of the investigation it is possible for the teacher to design provocative activities for the ITV environment. (In "Lights, Camera, Action" at the end of this chapter, we will give you an example of an activity from the French Connection, the two-way ITV pilot program that linked students in Paris, France, and Kansas, USA.)

The process of investigation involves asking questions and developing lines of reasoning; its by-product is conclusions. As is true of the inquiry approach in general, issue-based inquiry helps students acquire skills that allow them to design and perform investigations, arrive at generalizations, communicate their findings to others, and create new questions to launch further inquiries. During this process the direct connection between answers and questions is made.

Important Point: Be sure that the inquiry process provides questions for answers as well as answers to questions. Students learn better when the connection between the two is clear.

Although exploration and inquiry occur within a structure (usually determined by a set of leading questions), and are facilitated by the teacher and materials, students typically:

- pursue their own inquiries;
- create their own focus;
- discover new directions;
- reshape investigations; and
- work together for brainstorming, analysis, and drawing conclusions.

When we designed the materials for the French Connection we relied heavily on both the constructivist theory and the inquiry model. They promote interaction, which is key to successful instruction over ITV, and help mitigate the perception of distance between the classrooms (you'll find more detail on this in chapter 5).

Reflection: What techniques have you developed in your classroom that really get the students involved and interacting?

## ALIGNING CONTENT WITH STANDARDS

"Mommy, where did standards come from?"

In 1994, Congress passed legislation that redefined education as we know it in this country. At face value, the 1994 Improving America's School Act (IASA) was just a reauthorization of the Elementary and Secondary Education Act (ESEA), which provided federal funding for education. But what really happened was that IASA initiated a shift in "education consciousness" that is continuing to impact both the content and the assessment of instructional efforts.

Before 1994, there was a general feeling that the educational system had done its duty if it provided all children with equal education (which was taken to mean equal effort invested in each student). But IASA took the position that equal effort is not enough—that results are more important than equality of effort. Now, since the creation of IASA, the prevailing attitude is that all children, regardless of background, must meet predetermined standards that have been written by their respective school districts and states. In other words, if equal treatment isn't producing equal progress toward the standards, then schools are honor bound to increase their efforts until all students are up to standard.

Reflection: If all students are supposed to meet the standards, how does this affect your classroom instruction and relationships with your students?

The nationwide push for standards-based education has been tremendous. Although the degree of impact of IASA varies, most districts and states have determined standards and are working to improve their students' progress toward them. Even institutions of higher education are rethinking the content and process of instruction in order to determine consistent approaches.

Important Point: Because of IASA, it is crucial that all elements of education help students meet standards.

It is tempting, when teaching over an ITV system, to focus on fun and innovative instructional strategies instead of organizing the class around appropriate standards or requirements. (This is like an "everything is good for them" mentality.) It is definitely possible to use fun and innovative strategies in the context of standards-based education, but it takes teacher/staff time and effort, and most importantly, thinking and reflecting.

*You put your right foot in . . . you put your right foot out . . .*

The first thing you need to do is find a copy of the content and performance standards that address your grade level and/or subject area. It is possible that the standards you find might be too general to build on (general standards give you more flexibility, but you often have to break them down into subcategories to address more specific issues). Or you can combine standards to address a greater number of objectives, and make the instruction more efficient and interesting. (Thematic units make it easy to do this.)

For example, if you taught in beautiful Texas, you would have the "Texas Essential Knowledge and Skills" (TEKS). (By the way, Texas *is* beautiful, but ask a Texan, not a Coloradan. For years Colorado has hosted tomato wars against Texas in the Rocky Mountains. The tomato-stained casualties have been horrendous.)

The TEKS clarify what Texan students are expected to know and be able to do. Two of these requirements for 6th grade are "the student listens actively and purposefully in a variety of settings" and "the student communicates clearly."

Although these statements are fairly global, teachers can often clarify their meaning by looking at what the state assessment targets. To give an example, one way the state assessment measures TEKS is by testing how well students follow directions. It is also expected that the students be able to give directions.

If you had limited English speakers in your class, for instance, you could also address English as a Second Language (ESL) concerns by focusing on giving and receiving directions. Or this objective could be immersed in a content area, such as math or home economics (see the inquiry-based math lesson, below).

*You put your right foot in and you shake it all about . . .*

It is important to note that all instruction includes some hidden objectives as well as the targeted ones. These subtle objectives contain academic as well as social components. When planning the standards or objectives to be taught, you should also consider what hidden beliefs are also being taught. No instruction is value-free.

Caution: Be sure you are aware of everything you will be teaching—both the up-front objectives and those that are hidden.

To continue the above example, if you are designing a class around giving and receiving instructions, hidden objectives and beliefs could include:

| Hidden Objectives | Hidden Beliefs |
|---|---|
| ❖ using appropriate manners, <br> ❖ extending vocabulary, <br> ❖ following safety procedures, <br> ❖ using spatial perceptions, <br> ❖ improving penmanship, <br> ❖ enhancing questioning techniques, <br> ❖ increasing memory, <br> ❖ noticing detail, <br> ❖ drawing objects, <br> ❖ improving comprehension, <br> ❖ improving writing, etc. | ❖ it's not good to interrupt people, <br> ❖ asking is better than being lost, <br> ❖ being articulate improves your image, <br> ❖ not following directions is a crime, <br> ❖ strangers can be harmful, <br> ❖ learning is fun, <br> ❖ you do better on tests if you follow directions, <br> ❖ knowing English is the most important skill in the world, <br> ❖ different cultures are interesting. |

*You do the hokey pokey and you turn yourself about . . .*

Once you determine the standards and objectives you are addressing, you need to consider how you can meet them by using the pedagogy discussed previously. So, say that we have—

| Students: | 6th grade LEP math students. |
|---|---|
| Standards: | The student listens actively and purposefully in a variety of settings. |
| | The student communicates clearly. |
| Associated Standards: | Math as communication. |
| | Characteristics of geometric figures. |
| Objectives: | The student will be able to give good directions. |
| | The student will be able to follow directions. |
| Other/Obj.: | Students will understand the importance of clear directions. |
| | Students will have the appropriate vocabulary to give and receive directions. |
| | Students will be comfortable asking for directions. |
| | Students will be able to visualize directions. |
| | Students will be able to construct and follow a sequence. |
| | Students will notice detail. |
| | Students will respect themselves and each other. |

Then a possible inquiry-based lesson might look like this:

---

## What Does It Look Like?

### Inquiry-based Math Lesson

Leading Question: What makes some directions easier to understand and follow than others?

Earlier discussion has focused on the fact that math is a type of language that is used to communicate quantitative ideas and processes. Now the teacher facilitates a discussion about giving and following directions, and introduces the leading question.

She then tells the students that she is going to draw a geometric figure, and she is going to stop frequently so that they can explain to her the process she has just completed. As they explain she writes the steps on the board. Then she asks if the students have any questions about the figure. There are a variety of questions, which she answers and writes on the board.

Now she has a student from one of the remote sites come to the overhead camera in his classroom. Students at all sites have a piece of paper in front of them with a geometric figure drawn on it. Measurements are indicated for angles and sides. Class members take turns telling the student at the overhead camera how to draw the figure, sometimes with humorous results.

For homework or during lunch, the students are to give a picture of a geometric figure to a friend or parent (interviewee) and write down the directions that person gave for how to duplicate the figure (half of the students received one new figure and the other half another).

During the next day's class, the students (interviewers) share the various sets of directions in small groups and discuss such topics as:

- Did everyone approach the task the same way?
- What types of strategies were used?
- What vocabulary helped?
- Did following a sequence help?
- Was it easier if the interviewer asked questions?
- How did their interviewee help them visualize the figure?

The students then write down the most effective directions they can, using the insights they have gained. Each student gives the new directions to a student from the group that had been given the different figure for the homework assignment. Then the class discusses if there was any improvement.

---

"That's what it's all about!"

Using a constructivist approach with content that is aligned with standards does seem to take more energy and time than just following a workbook or telling the students "how it is." But if the students are not engaged and do not apply the learning to their own world, the time that is put in will fail to produce long lasting results and create the scholars we want. Besides, teaching bored students is usually boring to the teacher.

## CREATING A LEARNING COMMUNITY

Many educators (the authors of this book included) are aware that teaching over distance can deepen feelings of isolation for some students. We can't guarantee that this won't happen, but we can guarantee that with care, planning, and inventiveness it is possible to create a real learning community where you and your students flourish.

For one thing, multimedia tools give you a much broader range of possibilities for drawing reluctant students into interaction. For another, maintaining constant emphasis on interaction, both in planning and in the "classroom," will allow you to develop a community where cooperation and teaming are a necessary part of the learning environment.

 Important Point: The more students relate to each other and personalize the academic content, the better they learn.

Another way to create a learning community with ITV is to use the system for the benefit of the community at large. Possibilities abound for putting the ITV system to work in this way. You will be able to think of many more, but here are some examples of how you can do it:

- Community meetings
- Community education classes
- Continuing education classes
- Postsecondary degree programs
- Meetings in their primary language for parents of kids in bilingual programs
- Professional development for teachers and administrators

You can see that ITV learning communities don't have to be limited to those you create within your ITV classroom. In addition to the obvious benefits of using your school district's ITV system for community activities, using the system in this way also familiarizes parents and other community members with the work that their students are doing, and invites them to be part of it. This is a tremendous public relations tool.

## CHAPTER 3 KEY POINTS

1. The responsibility for keeping the instruction interactive falls on the teacher.
2. Talking heads are boring.
3. As the constructivist theory relies on interaction, it tends to work well as a pedagogy for interactive television.
4. Teacher as facilitator works better on ITV than teacher as presenter.
5. Application of the inquiry model allows you to take advantage of the distances that separate sites; that is, to treat distance as a positive component rather than a negative. The inquiry model also adds to the emphasis on interaction between sites and students.
6. As standards-based instruction is a major initiative for all school districts and some institutions of higher learning, all instruction over ITV should be geared toward predetermined standards and objectives.
7. Teachers need to consider not only identified objectives to be taught, but also those that are more subtle, as well as beliefs that are being promoted.
8. With brainstorming and reflection, lessons can be planned and implemented that are highly interactive, effective, and meet predetermined standards and objectives.
9. Good ITV instruction also depends on aligning the content of the teaching materials with standards that have been developed for your grade level and/or subject area.
10. It is possible to use fun and innovative themes and strategies within the context of defined standards, but it takes teacher/staff time and effort.
11. The first step is to familiarize yourself with the content and performance standards.

## LIGHTS, CAMERA, ACTION

So how do you go about creating a lesson that will work well (for example, engage your students and facilitate learning) over two-way interactive television? To help you begin, we will give you an example of a lesson from the French Connection that the students particularly enjoyed. The French Connection was a "World Geographic Problems" course with a basic pedagogy that relied on issue-based inquiry and the constructivist theory.

 Although dated, Francis Slater's *Learning through Geography* (1982) provided a solid foundation for the French Connection pedagogy. This is also a great resource for people who are just beginning to dabble in inquiry-based instruction.

Example Module: "How Do People Adapt To and Change Places?"

Background: This module (the first in the curriculum) was designed to break the ice. In addition to the obvious learning objectives, this first international hook-up between schools in France and the United States was intended to create a learning community: to help the students get to know and feel comfortable with each other via the technology of two-way interactive television.

The leading question for this particular lesson was "What kind of place do you live in?" Before the hook-up, students on both sides of the Atlantic came up with working definitions of neighborhood, and made sketch maps of their neighborhoods. The students in Paris included buildings, streets, city landmarks, etc., and in Kansas they included roads, property lines, buildings, and rural landmarks.

During the international hook-up the students showed their sketch maps to each other and exchanged information about their neighborhoods. They discussed how neighborhoods expand and change, and what mobility has to do with the concept of neighborhood. They started talking about where they lived and how they got around, and beyond even the most optimistic expectations for interaction, they started asking each other questions about transportation systems and how they differed from urban Paris to rural Kansas.

The students from Kansas were amazed at the sophisticated metro system in Paris, but the Parisians were even more amazed that the kids in Kansas drove around their world in pickup trucks. In talking about city and rural neighborhoods and transportation systems, they learned more about the cultural geography of each other's regions in 45 minutes than if they had spent hours reading textbooks. They not only forgot to be nervous about being on television, but they forgot that they were on television.

*Your Assignment:*

1. The first step in creating an interactive lesson for ITV is to come up with the leading question and a set of subquestions. Using the same example from the French Connection, here are the leading question and subquestions:

   What kind of place do you live in?
   What is a neighborhood?
   How has your neighborhood expanded in your life?
   How do you move around in your neighborhood?
   How does your transportation system affect your neighborhood?

   When questions are well structured, students are led step-by-step toward an understanding of the problem or idea that is being investigated. A hallmark of the inquiry method is that there is a clear link, from the onset, between the question being explored and the answer or conclusion that will be uncovered by the end of the lesson. Conclusions are not simply presented by the teacher, but arrived at during the process of inquiry into a specific question.

2. The best way to come up with leading questions and subquestions is to use the brainstorming technique. This is particularly effective if more than one person is participating, so if you have a team teacher or know another teacher who is teaching a similar class, brainstorm with her or him. If not, use the brainstorming technique on your own.

*Things to Remember about Brainstorming:*

- There are no dumb ideas.
- Think first of "big" general ideas.
- Use a flip chart to write down every idea that occurs—don't judge its worth.
- Once you've milked your brain(s) of general ideas (in this case, questions), look them over and select one that will point your students in the direction you'd like them to take. This will be the leading question.
- With the leading question in mind, brainstorm for subquestions that will lead students into the tasks of identification, definition, description, classification, and analysis that will help them explain and answer the "big" question.

# 4

# Getting Ready

**QUESTIONS TO PONDER:**

1. How can you be well prepared for your classes and still leave room for spontaneity?
2. How much can you borrow from already published materials without getting yourself in hot water?

It is possible to feel completely overwhelmed when faced with ITV technology and the myriad of new instructional possibilities that go along with it. The two best methods of controlling this condition are to plan each lesson carefully and to become proficient in the skills necessary for effective ITV instruction. This chapter will lead you through the steps necessary to prepare a lesson, and chapters 5 and 6 will focus on helping you acquire the new skills you'll need as an ITV teacher.

Important Point: The way to a successful lesson is to prepare, prepare, and prepare.

Research supports our observation that preparation for ITV classes takes more time than planning lessons for the traditional classroom. This could be due in part to the fact that cameras record and seem to exaggerate things like mistakes and dead time. It is entirely possible that face-to-face instruction has as many flaws, but we never see them without feedback from the cameras.

Important Point: In order to maximize student time on air, the teacher needs to spend more time before class in preparation.

The extra planning time necessary for ITV instruction is also due to the number of components that are involved when preparing for a lesson to be broadcast over the system.

Getting ready includes:

✓ Examining the knowledge and experiences the students bring to the class;
✓ Determining the most crucial missing knowledge and processes for the students;
✓ Double checking the alignment with standards or other predetermined guidelines;
✓ Organizing the information into an interesting and interactive lesson;
✓ Adding the media components (print, audio, and video) and support materials;
✓ Making sure all instructional and technical staff are together in their understanding of the procedure; and
✓ Making sure the equipment is functioning, and that students will be present at the appropriate sites with other operational duties completed.

## TEACHER AS DIRECTOR

After reading chapter 3 and completing the activities at the end, you might have ideas about the content you want to teach and the type of pedagogy that supports effective instruction over ITV. The next step is getting to know your students or audience. The success of your instruction depends on meeting the needs of your students, not just on the innovative technology.

Important Point: Know your students.

Student characteristics that need to be considered when tailoring your lesson or addressing individual styles:

- ❖ Student motivation;
- ❖ Academic levels;
- ❖ Learning styles;
- ❖ Student interests;
- ❖ Related experiences students are bringing to the class; and
- ❖ Qualities of student home life or culture

---

### What Does It Look Like?

Many programs have used one-page surveys or personal inventories to elicit the information described above. Other programs use a simple autobiography assignment that serves the same purpose, but can also segue into writing, history, psychology, etc.

---

When tailoring lessons to match students needs, Howard Gardner's multiple intelligences model is a good system for describing students' individualities. Basically, Gardner says that everyone has different innate abilities and ways of processing information (which he calls "intelligences"). Aligning instructional strategies with the different intelligences can support the acquisition of knowledge by the student.

For example, some students might learn a concept better by discussing the components in a group, while another might learn it better by creating a visual representation. Having the students identify and provide information about their types of intelligence might help you select strategies that will be more effective in your class. On page 54, we have aligned Gardner's intelligences with possible ITV strategies.

So what happens when you have a hundred or more students? How can you possibly address everyone's individual learning style and past experience?

We have found it to be so important to tailor instruction to the needs and experiences of the students that almost any effort in this direction is worthwhile. Even a one-page "bubble" survey that can be scanned quickly by the teacher gives a more complete picture of the students as a group and makes it possible to align the content accordingly. Discussions and examples can be adapted to the class "personality."

 Glossary: **bubble survey**—a survey in which responses are marked in small circles that can be read and tabulated by a scanner and computer.

| Intelligence | Description | ITV Activities for Students |
|---|---|---|
| Linguistic intelligence | The capacity to use words effectively, whether orally or in writing | Interviews and presentations by students over the system |
| Logical-mathematical intelligence | The capacity to use numbers effectively, to reason well and to engage in inductive and deductive thinking/ reasoning. | Gathering data over distance to analyze. |
| Visual/spatial intelligence | The sense of being able to visualize an object and ability to create internal mental images/ pictures. | Creating maps of sites visited by camera. |
| Body-kinesthetic intelligence | The awareness of physical movement and the knowing/wisdom of the body, and the ability to use one's hands to produce or transform things. | Science simulations shared over the system. |
| Musical/rhythmic intelligence | The ability to perceive, discriminate, transform, and express musical forms and a sensitivity to rhythm and beats. | Choral reading together by the different sites. |
| Interpersonal intelligence | The capacity to perceive and make distinctions in moods, intentions, motivations, and feelings of other people. | Team projects with students from different sites. |
| Intrapersonal intelligence | The awareness of inner states of being, self-reflection, metacognition (for example, thinking about thinking) and spiritual realities. | Journal follow-up to day's lesson over ITV; could be faxed to teacher. |

(Adapted from Howard Gardner's *Frames of Mind* (1983) to include the distance education component.)

Important Point: Try to become as familiar with your students' needs and learning styles as possible.

Reflection: Do our schools and institutions promote the idea of an "ideal" student? How does this perception fit into the research on learning styles?

## CREATING EXPANDED LESSON PLANS

The next step is to write the actual lesson plan. In the past, teachers have had some flexibility in determining the depth of detail of their lesson plans, or even deciding whether they were going to write lesson plans at all. Some lessons were considered simple or familiar enough that writing the plan ahead of time wasn't necessary. This attitude is definitely not applicable to ITV. A written lesson plan is crucial to your ITV instruction, whether or not you have technicians or site facilitators that need to follow along (see chapter 4).

Caution: You can't "wing it." Don't *even* try!

A simple format for organizing a lesson plan is given on page 56 (lesson template). The content is organized in chronological order from the beginning of the class to the end. The first column of the form displays the outline of your lesson content. This outline will include crucial questions, appropriate activities, student reflection, and time to synthesize and summarize new information. Strategies that emphasize interaction should be included here. Chapter 5 has a number of strategies to promote class engagement. Ways of measuring progress should also be noted in this column. Chapter 7 has suggestions and ideas on assessing students.

The first column should also include either verbal clues for alerting the technician that media support is now required, or a note to yourself that this is where the media support should be activated. In the second column, directly across from the clue or note, are listed the details of specific media support (see lesson template). Chapter 6 has ideas on creating and adapting media support. Media support could include charts, graphs, pictures, photographs, slides, video clips, audiotapes, etc. For example, an introductory movie clip on absolute and relative location would be noted directly across from the section of the outline that introduces the lesson (see lesson template). Without the correct notation, there is a danger of inserting media support at the wrong time.

Important Point: Be sure to take advantage of the media component.

## Example of an Expanded Lesson Plan (lesson template)

| Lesson Outline | Media Support |
|---|---|
| Topic: What are the absolute and relative locations of your city or town? | |
| Let's see *National Geographic's* definitions of absolute and relative location—Start film | Introductory film clip on Location Marker #3332-3301 |
| Discuss definitions from readings: | Alternate definition slides and map examples |
|   - location | |
|   - absolute location | |
|   - coordinate system | |
|   - fix | |
|   - line of position | |
|   - relative location | |
| How does this apply to your life?— Select students for activity | |
| Activity: | |
|   Students take turns in front of camera sharing the absolute and relative location of their birth place. | Students in front of camera, one at a time |
| Thank you, now let's look at our homework | |
| (Switch to character generator) | |
| Homework: | |
| In a world atlas, find out which are the biggest cities in the world, then locate each of them on a map. | Use character generator and atlas ten to display assignment |
|   - In what range of latitude do the cities occur? | |
|   - What is the average latitude? | |
|   - How many of the cities are located next to a body of water (ocean, lake, or river)? | |

*continued*

- Which of the above questions
  refer to absolute location and
  which to relative location?
  Activity:
Open questioning on "location"                    Camera on students
between sites:
  - Why does your family live where
    they do?
  -What are the advantages and
    disadvantages of your location?
  - Where would you live if you
    could live anywhere on earth?
    Why?
  - What is it like at your location?

Before the actual presentation of the lesson, the completed plan should be shared with other team members such as the technicians or site facilitators. If possible (especially in the beginning of the year or semester), a practice run of the lesson should be timed.

 Caution: Do not go beyond your scheduled time. It interferes with other classes and makes your students antsy. (Many computerized systems are programmed to end the lesson automatically.)

If it is not possible to time the lesson, the planning done before the instruction should guarantee that it will not run beyond the predetermined time. Holding classes beyond their allotted time can result in an abrupt cutting off of the picture, or in student revolution.

What if you have a great lesson prepared with all media support easily accessible and there is no picture or sound?

Chapter 2 described troubleshooting with the equipment, but as far as instruction is concerned, you need to be prepared in case your link with the students has disappeared. (Of course, it is easier to avoid problems if you take time before every class to check out all of the equipment.) But if the equipment does fail, you should keep a back-up lesson handy that is independent of the system and can be used if you can't reach your students at the remote sites. Every site should have a copy of the lesson with the necessary materials. Even with the best of systems, glitches that stop your wonderfully planned lessons will occur.

Important Point: Always have a back-up lesson ready in case the system doesn't work.

---

**What Does It Look Like?**

When the fiber optic cable was cut by an out-of-bounds construction worker, the site facilitators moved into action and passed out directions and materials that had been previously designed for this very possibility. The content of the lesson matched the course's content and relied on researching at the library and interviewing other students with experience in the area. Each facilitator then had one of the students lead a discussion on the topic while another student recorded the findings. The findings were then summarized to be shared with the other sites during the next class (which, in this case, was not scheduled until the following week).

---

## COPYRIGHT DOS AND DON'TS

Teachers have always felt relatively free to borrow ideas and materials for the sake of good instruction. And up until the advent of electronic media, we generally didn't have to worry about the legality of using pieces of other people's work for the education of our students. These days, however, the popular practice of blithely copying computer software and videotapes has called so much attention to copyright issues that such naivete is no longer sustainable.

---

### Read all about it!
# Copyright Issues Strike Fear into the Hearts of Educators!

_____          _____

_____          _____

_____          _____

_____          _____

_____          _____

_____          _____

Glossary: **copyright**—exclusive rights to the ownership and distribution of a particular literary, musical, artistic, or dramatic work for a specified amount of time. Copyright doesn't protect a work from being used by others; it just protects it from being copied in its entirety.

Unfortunately, because ITV is a broadcast medium that is closely related to commercial television, the educational copyright issues involved are particularly slippery and open to misinterpretation. Part of the problem is that classes taught over ITV are so much more visible, in a general sense, than classes taught behind the closed door of a traditional classroom. Teachers doing business as usual (synthesizing new materials out of a combination of their own original work and other pre-existing materials) might not realize that in transmitting these new materials over television, they make themselves vulnerable to copyright violations.

Another part of the problem is that in the relatively unexplored arena of educational technology, no one seems to know exactly what constitutes a copyright violation and what doesn't. Many of the guidelines used by teachers in the past no longer apply, and it's easy to find yourself swimming in murky waters if you aren't well informed. What all of this boils down to is the possibility of higher costs (both in money and time) for the planning and implementation of ITV instruction.

Important Point: Be careful of what you borrow.

When, exactly, do copyright issues apply to you and what you're planning to teach over the system?

- Any time you use prerecorded material (such as music from a tape or CD, or a segment from videotape) in a lesson that will be broadcast over the system.
- Any time you broadcast or distribute already published written materials, illustrations, or photographs.

Because this is such a very complicated problem (we won't say hopeless!), our aim is to familiarize you with the basic issues rather than provide comprehensive coverage of them. But because you will need to understand copyright issues before producing materials for your own classes, we refer you to the books listed in Appendix A (see the section on copyright).

## Fair Use

Because teachers have always used (and always will) wonderful bits and pieces from great literary, musical, and dramatic works to support their lessons, there are special "fair use" provisions of copyright laws that apply to educational situations. Basically, "fair use" limits copyright holders' monopolies on their copyrighted works. What this means to you is that there are some cases in which you can legally borrow material for presentations over ITV. For instance, academic (nonperformance) use of recorded music is allowed, provided that you use excerpts only, and no more than ten percent of the whole work. This provision allows you to use appropriate music to accompany presentations. However, closed circuit transmissions (including ITV) of copyrighted material are only permissible within *one* building, and not *between* buildings (figure that one out!). This is a good example of the above-mentioned murkiness of copyright issues, and it lends substance to our recommendation that you go ahead and obtain written permission for all copyrighted material used in your lessons.

Glossary: **fair use**—provisions of copyright laws that allow people to use limited selections of copyrighted works.

According to copyright law there are four tests used to ascertain whether use of copyrighted material falls within the "fair use" provision. The following checklist will help you stay within the law when you create materials for lessons (Hutchings-Reed in Willis, ed., 1994; and Cyrs and Smith, 1990).

*Fair Use Checklist*

- Is your use of copyrighted materials for commercial or for nonprofit educational purposes?
- Are specific limitations determined by the nature of the copyrighted work (depending on whether it is written on paper or recorded on some other medium such as film, diskette, etc.)?
- Are you using 10 percent or less of the copyrighted material?
- Is your use going to affect the potential market for or value of the copyrighted work?

(Willis, ed., 1994)

Before we leave the topic of copyright behind, let us repeat that you really need to explore this issue in depth before you make important decisions about use of copyrighted materials. The bottom line is that it never hurts to seek permission, and when permission is granted be sure to give copyright credit on written copies or in the credits of films, videotapes, etc. Be aware that using copyrighted materials for broadcast or transmission has its own set of problems, and it pays to become familiar with them.

Important Point: Even when selections are public domain, be sure to give the creators credit.

Reflection: To what degree do copyright laws protect the authors or artists? Do you think the copyright limitations are too stringent for ITV?

## CHAPTER 4 KEY POINTS

1. For most people, planning for ITV classes takes more time than planning for the traditional classroom.
2. Teaching over interactive television involves more external dimensions that need attention than in the traditional classroom.
3. In order to tailor instruction and encourage interaction, it is important to know your students in greater detail than is currently the norm.
4. A well thought out, chronologically written lesson plan is crucial for effective ITV instruction.
5. The lesson plan outline needs to clearly link the content being covered to the appropriate media support.
6. Back-up lesson plans are always a good idea in case of system failure.
7. Copyright laws are more stringent over video networks.
8. As copyright laws are not always clear, it is important for teachers to research both national guidelines and local practices.
9. Often asking permission from authors or artists is easier than trying to identify what can be used and what can't.

## LIGHTS, CAMERA, ACTION

1. Using ideas developed from chapter 1 through chapter 3, and the lesson plan template on page 56, write a lesson plan following the procedure given in this chapter.
2. Find your institution's guidelines (or your school board policy) on the use of copyrighted materials, or if none exist, get together with other ITV teachers in your school or institution and develop a policy paper.

# 5

# So Far and Yet So Near

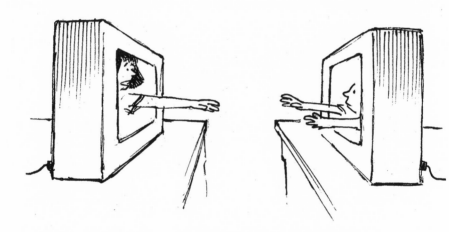

**QUESTIONS TO PONDER:**

1. Is it possible to take the "remoteness" out of your remote sites?
2. How can you make interaction happen among students who are "present" to each other only as images and sounds on a television screen?

Think about what the word "distance" means, and how many different ways we use it. There's distance in space (I live on the other side of town from Ralph); distance in time (I live fifteen minutes from Ralph's house); and emotional or psychological distance (Ralph who?).

One of the greatest challenges you will face in your ITV classroom is finding a way to deal with all three types of distance. But you might find, as a teacher with state-of-the-art technology at your fingertips, that psychological distance is harder to overcome than the first two put together. Whatever your school's ITV system consists of, distance in time and space will mostly be taken care of by the equipment (barring mechanical failure). But how about the *feeling* of distance? Technology will only bring your class together on an emotional/psychological level if you constantly focus on creating a cohesive, interrelated group.

## TEACHER AS CONDUCTOR

In chapter 3, "What to Teach and How to Teach It," we focused on pedagogy, and asked you to redefine your concept of the classroom. Even further, we asked you to step out of the role of "voice of authority" and become a fellow explorer, along with your students. Now we are asking you to move into yet another mind-set.

Think of yourself as the conductor of a symphony orchestra. Your job is a dynamic one, and whether you're the flamboyant type or more reserved, it involves keeping attention focused, controlling the pace and timing, and bringing out or subduing the various players at appropriate times.

The students are the players: the violinists' part weaves in and out of each movement; the French horns appear here and there; the guy on the kettledrum only shows up at the end—but then he practically knocks everyone out of their seats. Which of these players is more important? The conductor's job is to create a sense of relationship among all of them, and to coax the music out of each one.

There are many ways to do this, and most, if not all of them, will already be familiar to you from your traditional classroom. The strategies discussed below focus on decreasing distance by creating dynamic, cooperative relationships among the players in your ITV classroom.

## AGGRESSIVE INTERACTION

The reason we use the word "aggressive" in this context is not because we want you to promote aggressive behavior (*au contraire!*). But we honestly believe that the only way to create a successful and exciting ITV classroom is to become a fanatic where interaction is concerned. Not only is interaction one of the best known antidotes for the talking head syndrome, but it also significantly increases students' ability to learn.

### Real-time Interaction

In 1994 a researcher observed corporate training that used a mixture of audio and video materials but no interaction. When he introduced real-time interactivity, the retention rate of the corporate trainees increased from about 20 percent to about 75 percent (Millbank in L. Sherry, 1996).

It is worth pointing out that interaction doesn't have to be limited to real-time. As mentioned in chapter 2, knowledge building can happen through interaction both in the classroom and outside of it (for example, by using the Internet to create an electronic bulletin board system for your class).

Reflection: What type of strategies have you used in the past that encouraged interaction between yourself and your students?

## STRATEGIES THAT PROMOTE INTERACTION

There are a number of teaching strategies that increase interactivity between the teacher and students, and among the students themselves. These strategies can be grouped into the following five categories:

- Strategies that develop interaction through interpersonal relationships;
- Strategies that use questioning activities to improve interaction and learning;
- Strategies that use real-life people and places to engage the students in interactive learning;
- Strategies that use drama to create the interaction; and
- Strategies that emphasize the use of collaborative learning groups through interactive activities.

### Developing Interaction through Interpersonal Relationships

*Establishing Rapport*

How do you establish rapport with your students? Here are a few ideas:

- Don't worry about making a fool of yourself—your students will also be feeling foolish.

- Start each class with an attention getter or icebreaker, especially in the beginning.
- Laughter brings people together—use humor as often as possible.
- CONSTANTLY PROMOTE INTERACTION!
- Self-confidence (your own and that of your students) comes with practice and experience. Work at maintaining confidence.
- Be flexible and learn to cope with the inevitable changes that are going to jump out and surprise you.
- Creativity and spontaneity are essential—be willing to play.
- Avoid excess verbiage—do more showing, asking, and interacting.
- Change the pace.
- Remember that ITV magnifies dead time and weaknesses in your presentation.
- Get all the students together so that they can make personal contact. This should happen as soon after classes begin as possible, and be repeated as often as possible.

Glossary: **dead time**—intervals when nothing is happening.

*Humanize your ITV Classroom*

Because teaching students over two-way interactive television is, by definition, an exercise in distance education, it is necessary to create an environment that promotes genuine human contact and learning experiences. The following strategies will help you do that.

---

### What Does It Look Like?

**Be a human being, yourself:**

- Write welcome letters to all students before school begins;
- Don't be afraid of self-disclosure—let the students know who you are;
- Use personal vignettes (good for rapport, stressing a concept, making content more interesting)—might use props, should be fairly short, and best if related to the subject being discussed or used as icebreakers;
- Don't offend anyone, but let your ham take over;
- Bring in personal tokens (photographs, mementos, etc.);
- Write personal notes to students on papers you're handing back; and
- Be sure students at the remote and home sites are getting equal attention (see Keeping Track of Turns, p. 70).

---

Important Point: Have students create name signs for their desks, and create one for your own. Especially in the beginning, it is hard for the teacher and students to remember all the names at all the sites.

## Making Introductions

The most crucial time for establishing yourself as a "real" person, and for creating a "people-oriented" interactive environment, is during the first few weeks of the course. Introducing the people participating in the class, as well as describing the structure of the class, is crucial for later interaction. Look at the top of page 68 for some ideas on making introductions.

Caution: Don't skimp on introduction time at the beginning of the year. It is very important that the students feel they know you and each other.

Reflection: Do you find it easy or hard to quickly develop relationships with people? Is it possible to connect for the sake of teaching, even if you are a shy person?

**What Does It Look Like?**

**Spend time on introductions**

- Even if you think you have a tight schedule, be willing to spend two or more class sessions just getting to know one another;
- Use the following introduction activity (or one of your own):
  - Have students at each of the sites pair off and interview each other (you will pair with a student at the home site),
  - Each member of the pair will interview the other, collecting information to present to the class;
  - Pairs at each site will introduce each other over the system (you should go first);
- As a way of a personal introduction, have each student present an introductory collage at the teacher station, using several cameras:
  - The collage can be made up of photos, magazine words, and images, etc.
  - The presenting student will use the overhead camera to show the collage, one camera on him(her)self, and possibly one of the remote cameras to introduce a friend; and
- Use the mnemonic activity:
  - Give a homework assignment for each participant (including yourself) to think of a short mime or charade that that will help everyone remember each other's name (see The First Day, page 79),
  - Have each participant present her mnemonic device, starting with your own.

## Using Questioning Activities

*Ask Students for Feedback*

One way of keeping your students engaged is to provide and ask for feedback; this is especially helpful for reeling in students who might have a tendency to drift away (especially at the remote sites). If a student seems disengaged to you, try the following exercise.

**What Does It Look Like?**

**Feedback Capsules**

Ask a student to spend one minute encapsulating what has been going on in the class-room. You can create your own rules for what should be in the feedback capsules (depending on the age of your students); either the student can give a general resume of information, or you can create a specific formula (like one major theme or two sub-themes or four identifying words, etc.). If the first student can't "fill" the capsule, any other student(s) at the same site can take over.

*Questioning*

In a recent study, university instructors were observed to see how much class time they spent asking and fielding questions. We are sorry to report that the observed instructors spent just a little more than two minutes of a 60-minute class engaged in questioning activities. Sadly, teleclass instructors were only slightly better (Cyrs and Smith, 1990).

This is a tragic example of the virulence of the talking head syndrome, and really—you must not let this happen to you! Fortunately for all of our ITV students, there are a number of reasonably straightforward alternatives to the lecture approach, and most of them focus on promoting interaction. One option is to foster an atmosphere in which questions can (and do) flow in any direction.

Important Points: In addition to structuring your classes around leading questions and subquestions, be prepared with other questions pertinent to the day's material. It is important to include both *closed questions* and *open questions*.

---

### What Does It Look Like?

| Closed Questions (Recall) | | | Open Questions (High-level thinking) |
|---|---|---|---|
| How many pairs of shoes do you have? | Can you list them according to type (dressy, athletic, sandals, etc.)? | Is there a relationship between a person's income and the number of shoes he owns? | What conclusions can you draw by comparing the number of shoes in your closet with those owned by Prince Charles? |

---

Glossary: **closed question**—a question having a fixed answer.

Glossary: **open question**—a question with a speculative answer that encourages the student to reflect and investigate beyond the information given.

---

**Words of Wisdom**

- Ask a high-level question, get a high-level answer.
- Don't ask what you already know and don't tell what you can ask.
- Discussion should, by its nature, allow for more than one answer.
- When questioning, observe ground rules: use names, preplan visual and/or audio support, match questions to objectives, include wait time.

---

*Keeping Track of Turns*

It is crucial that you make a consistent effort to bring the students at your remote sites into the action. Here are two ways to guarantee that all your students will get equal attention.

---

**What it looks like**

- Write each student's name on a 3x5 card and call on each one in order until you've gone through the whole deck; shuffle and start over.
- Xerox a seating chart that includes all the sites in your classroom, and use a new one (or a new color to mark them) each day. Put a checkmark by a student's name as you call on her. Don't call on her again until the rest have checkmarks.

---

Important Point: Find a way of keeping track of turns. Most of us have a tendency to call on the same students (that is, those who are engaged and enthusiastic) over and over again.

## Using Real-Life People and Places

All students are more interested in learning when the materials are relevant and meaningful, and these two characteristics are obviously related. If learning materials are "real" to a student, he will probably be able to interact with them in a way that has meaning for him.

In chapter 3 we discussed "issue-based inquiry," in which learning is centered on an investigation into a real-world case study. Although there are never any guarantees, focusing learning materials on real-life situations goes a long way toward ensuring that they will be both relevant and meaningful.

*Fieldtrips and Interviews*

Other ways to satisfy the "relevancy criterion" include designing learning experiences that occur outside the scope of class materials, or bringing local activities into the ITV classroom. Fieldtrips and interviews can meet both of these needs, and can bring the real world into school in such a way that students experience the relationship between the two kinds of learning.

Once again, the multimedia possibilities of the ITV system greatly expand your options for creating fieldtrips and interviews. Instead of being limited to real-time, for example, these activities can be prerecorded and then shared over the system (as in the example from the French Connection on page 73). Fieldtrips and interviews can also occur as special events available through satellite downlinks, or they can occur online and be accessed by computer (see the Electronic Field-trip box at the top of page 72). Of course, technology can also help you broadcast real-time interviews from any of your ITV classroom sites.

Important Point: All communities are rich in human resources and subjects for interviews . . . use them!

Guest speakers can be invited to any of the sites during class time, and inter-viewed by students (who have been provided with background information on the speaker and have come prepared with questions).

Caution: It is very easy for one group to dominate an interview. Create a system that rotates to each site and allows students there to ask questions.

Glossary: **electronic fieldtrip**—a fieldtrip made available to students either through a satellite downlink, interactive televi-sion, or online using a computer.

Reflection: What are some local human and geographic resources that could be used for your classes?

## Using Culturally Relevant Content

One of the ways to help students experience a sense of ownership is to create learning materials from their own familiar worlds. The example at the bottom of page 72 is from the Navajo Distance Learning System in Window Rock, Arizona.

## Student Presentations

As mentioned above, students learn better when they feel responsible for their learning and actively participate in the learning process. One of the best ways to

---

**What Does It Look Like?**

**Electronic Fieldtrips: The JASON Project**

The JASON Project was founded by Dr. Robert Ballard in response to thousands of letters he received from students after he discovered the wreck of the Titanic. The project mounts virtual scientific expeditions to locations all over the world, as well as providing excellent professional development for teachers.

*Live Satellite and Internet Broadcasts*—The first two weeks of an expedition are broadcast to students at Primary Interactive Network Sites (PINS). An advanced telecommunications technology called Telepresence makes it possible for students at PINS to view the expedition live and interact with project scientists.

*JASON Online Systems*—Using the Internet, students can plug in to news and discussion groups, or participate in gathering data for local investigations. The JASON Project web site (www.jasonproject.com) also contains graphics, video and sound clips, and interactive exercises for students who have taken part (or are interested) in JASON expeditions.

JASON Project expeditions include:

* Making the first human observations of hydrothermal events in the Mediterranean Sea;
* Following the footsteps of Charles Darwin to the Galapagos Islands; and
* Studying the rain forest canopy and barrier reef in Belize to diagnose the health of our planet.

---

engage students in their own learning is to have them make presentations. Because of the multimedia possibilities inherent in the system, there are lots of snazzy options for student presentations over ITV that might or might not be available in the traditional classroom.

---

**What Does It Look Like?**

**Coyote Stories**

The coyote plays an important role within Navajo cosmology. Among other things he is known as the Trickster, and part of his role is to inject humor into the learning experience. The students in an ITV class that was broadcast from Window Rock, Arizona, collected coyote stories from their communities and took turns telling them over the system. Each student was then asked to make up her/his own coyote story, and these stories were also shared over the system. Not only did the stories hold the interest of the Navajo students, but they also honored their backgrounds and life experiences. Adding their own stories to the learning process encouraged them to be active learners.

---

The following example is from a two-week module that was created for the French Connection. The module focused on the geographic concept of regions and was entitled "Political Boundaries: How Does Political Change Affect Regions?"

---

**Student Video Presentations**

Preparation:

Students of Mlle. Michelle Prieur's geography class in Saint German en Laye are planning a field trip to Normandy this spring. During their trip they will make a video recording of the 50th Anniversary Celebration of the Normandy Landing. They will be documenting a part of what this major event in World War II meant to the people in this part of France.

At the same time students in the World Geographic Problems class in Kansas will be doing video interviews of their grandparents and other members of their community who participated in World War II. Some of the same events of the war will be remembered and recounted from very different perspectives. Both sets of students will edit their videos down to 15 minutes, or show only part of their videos.

Hook-up:

Approximately 30 minutes of the hook-up will be spent watching the video presentations. That should leave time for discussion after both videos have been shown. This is a unique opportunity to view the same historical event from different perspectives, as well as to try to reach generalizations and come to conclusions.

**Suggested Discussion Questions:**

How did these events affect political boundaries in Europe? How was the war different for people living in France than for American military personnel? How about non-military personnel living in the United States? How have those events impacted the lives of people 50 years later?

---

## Using Drama to Create Interaction

Caution: Many activities in this category engage students on an emotional level. Always allow time before the end of class for them to process their thoughts and feelings.

### Role Playing

Almost everyone loves a drama. Role playing is like improvisational theater, directed by a teacher who creates a structure that ties the drama into learning objectives. We have borrowed from the French Connection curriculum once again for the following example, which is from a lesson that focused on sustainable development on the island of Borneo. The two-week module was entitled "How Does Development Affect People and Places?"

Glossary: **simulation**—modeling of a real life process (physical or social) with variables that can be explored and changed, using either a computer model or an interactive process among the students.

---

**What Does It Look Like?**

**Mock Trial of a Penan Tribesperson**

Background:

Students have been working on this module for two weeks and have learned that the Penan are a forest-dwelling people who live in the tropical rainforests of Borneo. As a result of their investigation, students have learned that the Penan are being forced out of their homelands by an economic activity that is causing large-scale and rapid destruction of the rainforest while bringing great wealth to a small number of people. In addition to their investigations into the economic development of Malaysian rainforests, students have watched video clips of a famous trial.

Preparation:

Students will be given role cards describing roles they are to play in the trial. Roles include:

- Defendant (A member of the Penan tribe in Borneo who has sabotaged and destroyed a piece of heavy equipment belonging to a multinational logging corporation.)
- Defense attorney
- Prosecuting attorney
- Judge
- Witnesses for the defense and prosecution
- Members of the jury

The Trial:

To make the trial realistic, students playing the roles of judge and jury will adhere to biases that exist in this situation. The trial must reflect the prevailing reality of rain forest development in Malaysia. It will be very important for students to stick to their roles and not make decisions based on their own sense of fairness.

Debriefing:

This exercise is likely to stir up emotions, especially if the outcome of the trial is blatantly unfair. It will be important to allow time for students to reflect on and discuss the outcome of the trial, air their feelings, and reach conclusions.

---

*Simulations*

Although the term "simulation" often refers to the type of role-playing activity described above, we are narrowing it down to refer to activities in which real-world processes are simulated in the classroom. This can be done with computers (either using software designed for the purpose or creating computer models in class), or by creating situations in the classroom that simulate real processes. An example of the latter is building a covered terrarium that simulates biological and meteorological processes. In this case, plants release water vapor into the air through transpiration, and changing temperatures cause the vapor to condense into water and rain inside the closed terrarium. In the ITV environment, simulations can be enhanced by multimedia support (for example, slides, video clips, or music), and interactivity can be designed around simulations (discussions and presentations).

Survival Simulations: It is also possible to simulate social processes. Since their popularization in the 1970s, survival simulations have been used to give students a hands-on experience of cooperative problem solving, and to demonstrate the effectiveness of group work. The ITV classroom is a great proving ground for this type of work. Not only does it support interaction within small groups at each site, but the medium of television allows work done separately by each group to be presented to the students at all the other sites. The following activity is a typical survival simulation.

---

### What Does It Look Like?

**Shipwreck**

Each small group is told to imagine that it is the crew of a ship that is sinking off the coast of a tropical island. Limited space in the lifeboat requires that only eight items be taken off the ship for survival on the island.

The group must create a list, rank ordering the items with regard to the importance of each one to the group's survival.

The developer of this simulation (Jay Hall) also provides a list that was prepared by survival experts. This "master list" can be compared to 1) lists made by individual students, and 2) those generated by student groups. The point is clear when the group lists turn out to score higher than those created by individuals.

(Morris in Cohen, 1986)

---

An ITV variation of this activity would allow the entire ITV classroom (after each group has presented its list) to consolidate the separate lists into one that is agreed on by all the students in the class. The norms described on page 77 can be used first in each small group, and finally during the compilation of the class list.

### Interactive Games

The same games that work well in the traditional classroom will also work over the system. Here is an example.

## What Does It Look Like?

### Shares (An Interactive Game)

This game is designed to give students a first-hand experience of the unevenness of economic development. Have the students at each site count off in fours. The *ones* are from the United States, the *twos* are from Romania, the *threes* from Nicaragua, and the *fours* from Ethiopia. Each student will receive shares according to the country he lives in. The shares stand for per capita GNP (represented by M&Ms, nuts, etc.), life expectancy (represented by minutes of playing time), and availability of resources (represented by resource points).

The shares are distributed like this:

| COUNTRY | GNP (M&Ms, nuts, etc.) | LIFE EXPECTANCY | RESOURCE AVAILABILITY |
|---------|------------------------|-----------------|-----------------------|
| U.S.A. | 18 | 12 min. | 584 points |
| Romania | 9 | 11 min. | 120 points |
| Nicaragua | 4 | 9 min. | 22 points |
| Ethiopia | 1 | 6 min. | 1 point |

The point of the game is to beg, borrow, or negotiate for food and/or resource points. The teacher announces when the lifetime of each group is up. Allow class time for reflection and discussion after the game: What sorts of feelings did students have about the distribution of shares? Were they successful in getting more? Was there any visible difference between the attitudes of the "haves" as compared to the "have-nots"?

## Using Collaborative Groups

*Cooperative Learning/Collaborative Groups*

Because encouraging collaborative work is an essential part of interactive teaching, most, if not all, of the above strategies directly promote cooperative learning. Building relationships in your ITV classroom—giving students a chance to learn by talking and working together—is a specific and constant focus of interactive teaching. And even though you are dealing with students who are physically separated by distance, you can use the system to foster cooperative learning.

The "jigsaw activity" allows you to use the existing organization of your students according to site location. Here is how it works.

## What Does It Look Like?

### Jigsaw Activity

Assign the students at each site one part of an article, book, film, history lesson, etc., and have them discuss and learn only the part that has been assigned to their group. Keep track of which group is doing which piece, and call on groups in order when presentations are made. The idea is not only for each group to teach its own piece, but to learn that the whole is greater than the sum of its parts. After all the presentations have been made, facilitate a discussion about how students' perceptions changed after they became familiar with the entire piece.

In the 1970s, a body of research was developed that used creative problem solving to show that people working in groups generally come up with more effective solutions to problems than do individuals working by themselves (as in the survival simulation, above). A particularly useful tool emerged from this research:

> ## What Does It Look Like?
>
> *Norms:* **Student Guidelines for Cooperative Problem Solving**
>
> - Say your own ideas.
> - Listen to others; give everyone a chance to talk.
> - Ask others for their ideas.
> - Give reasons for your ideas and discuss many different ideas.
>
> (Morris in Cohen, 1986)

Important Point: Be sure to make full use of the site facilitators when you are focusing on cooperative activities.

## Peer Teaching

As we all know, one of the best ways to learn something is to teach it. (According to an old saw, we remember 5 percent of what we hear, and 90 percent of what we teach.) As in the traditional classroom, peer teaching is likely to involve paired groups in which the students interact one-on-one as teacher/learner. A good model to remember is one commonly used in medical schools: "Show one, do one, teach one."

## Debates

Sometimes, especially when a topic has generated controversy, it is useful to go beyond informal class discussion and stage a formal debate (the operative word, when dealing with a debate, is formal). Since a debate is a regulated discussion between two teams, it is necessary to begin with a set of rules. These rules can be strict tournament rules, or another set of rules that has been agreed on in advance. In the ITV environment the easiest way to form teams is to have the students at each site make up one team. It is possible to "mix and match" teams out of students from different sites, but this will obviously be more complicated.

*Brainstorming*

We've already mentioned the brainstorming technique with reference to teacher planning and leading questions. Brainstorming is also an excellent interactive tool for you to use with your students in the ITV classroom. Review the "Things to Remember About Brainstorming" in the "Lights, Camera, Action" section of chapter 3, and modify them for student brainstorming sessions.

Reflection: How good are the teaming skills of the adults that you work with or know socially? Do you feel that as educators we spend enough time on teaching students to work collaboratively?

---

**What Does It Look Like?**

**Debate: Hamlet Was a Wimp**

English Literature Class

1. The judge introduces the proposition and gives a brief background summary (for example, "Hamlet's reluctance to take action against his uncle and mother doesn't necessarily mean he was a wimp . . . it might have been because he loved them, didn't have enough confidence in himself." and so on). The judge will also be responsible for keeping the debate on track.
2. Because the affirmative team has the burden of proof, it goes first and last. The first speaker of the affirmative team opens with an argument that supports the proposition ("Hamlet was a wimp because _____").
3. The first speaker of the opposing team, having taken notes during the affirmative team's presentation, "attacks" the affirmative team's argument.
4. The second speaker of the affirmative team counters the opposing team's attack.
5. The second speaker of the opposing team presents that team's final argument.
6. The affirmative team summarizes its position, answering the final argument of the opposing team.
7. Either the judge or the class as a whole votes on the outcome of the debate. Make it clear to students that they should vote for the team that presented the best argument, not the one they happened to agree with.

## THE FIRST DAY

First days are usually very busy and might be a little crazy. It's important to get off to a good start.

✓ Do you have a plan to get to know everyone's name quickly and to balance turns?
✓ Do you have a packet for each student that has a syllabus, a schedule, an interactive study guide (page 31), and a list of outside resources?
✓ Do you have copies of your transparencies or any other visuals that the students would find helpful?
✓ Do you have the entire session carefully planned with contingencies for problems with the system (see chapter 2 and 4)?
✓ Are you making a backup tape so someone who missed the session can watch it at a better time?
✓ Do you have contracts ready for students to sign?
✓ Have you defined consequences for breaking the contracts?
✓ Are you prepared to discuss your and the students' expectations?

Caution: Be sure to let the students at your remote sites know that they aren't invisible. When introducing the system, mention that you can focus in on them and record them at any time without their knowing it.

## CHAPTER 5 KEY POINTS

• One of your greatest challenges as an ITV teacher is to take the *distance* out of distance learning.
• As an orchestrator, you have to be able to focus attention, regulate the pace, and facilitate the participation of each and every player.
• Because ITV is a high tech medium, it is important to humanize the learning environment—help create relationships among all the players in your classroom.
• One way of keeping your students engaged is to ask them for feedback. This is helpful for reeling in students who might have a tendency to drift away from the class activity (especially at the remote sites).

## What Does It Look Like?

### New Beginnings Scenario

The system is up and running, and today is Ms. Fulana's debut for teaching biology (or any other subject) over a two-way interactive television system. Among many other preparations, she has come armed with a seating chart that will allow her to call on each student by name.

| Site 1 | Tansy | Jesse | Chris | Star | Todd |
|--------|-------|-------|-------|------|------|
| Site 2 | Jessica | Victor | Donald | James | |
| Site 3 | Alena | Patricia | Mabel | Lena | |
| Site 4 | Charley | Sally | Susan | Michael | Kurt |

Ms. Fulana talks about herself for a while—her interest and experience in biology—and uses the overhead camera to show the students some photographs and other artifacts related to the subject.

Ms. Fulana then briefly discusses the class syllabus, the hows and whys of the equipment, (including a "Things Not to Do With ITV Equipment" list), and other administrative details.

## THINGS NOT TO DO WITH ITV EQUIPMENT

- ✓ Don't tap the microphones.
- ✓ Don't yell into the microphones.
- ✓ Don't make any more noise than necessary.
- ✓ Don't do anything that you'd be embarrassed to show friends or family on a videotape.
- ✓ Don't use any of the equipment without express permission.
- ✓ Don't be complacent if there is no picture or sound.

She has decided to use a mnemonic activity to introduce the students to herself and each other, and get them used to being on camera and communicating over the system. The students were told beforehand that they would be pantomiming their names, so they are prepared with short mimes or skits.

One of the students walks up in front of the camera, wads up a large piece of paper, and throws it at the students sitting down. He then says, "Every time you see me in front of the camera just remember, Don Truitt (threw it)." The class laughs and he gives a few sentences about his interests and sits down.

1. One of the best ways to guarantee interaction is to foster an atmosphere in which questions can (and do) flow in any direction; it is important to give class time to questions that range from closed to open.
2. Active learning gives students a sense of ownership of their own learning process. ITV students are more willing to invest effort in the learning process when the learning materials are relevant and meaningful; focusing learning materials on real-life situations goes a long way toward ensuring that they will be both.
3. One way to promote active learning (and satisfy the "relevancy criterion") is to engineer learning experiences that occur outside the scope of class materials, or to bring local activities into the ITV classroom. Fieldtrips and interviews can perform these functions.
4. Students learn better when they feel responsible for their learning and actively participate in the process. Student presentations are easy to incorporate into an ITV classroom.
5. Interactivity (including the connectivity that happens with interaction) is the single most vital element in the ITV classroom. Important interactive teaching tools include debates, role playing, simulations, and interactive games.
6. Encouraging collaborative work is an essential part of interactive teaching; building relationships should be a specific and constant focus of an ITV teacher.
7. Problem solving, peer teaching, debates, and brainstorming are all excellent tools for doing collaborative group work.

## LIGHTS, CAMERA, ACTION

If you have been doing the work in the "Lights, Camera, Action" sections at the end of each chapter, by now you have almost completed a lesson plan for your ITV class. In chapter 3 you created leading questions and subquestions around which to focus an inquiry; in chapter 4 you created a lesson plan and investigated copyright issues. Your work for this chapter is the following:

1. Using the inquiry you created in chapter 3, and expanding on the lesson plan you worked on in chapter 4, invent and write down an idea for a debate, a role-playing activity, or an interactive game.
2. Do whatever research is necessary to create a complex, multifaceted activity. Write the activity down in steps.
3. No matter which of the above activities you choose, use index cards to create "role cards" for the students who will participate (even the debate has different parts to be played).
4. Explain the activity in detail to someone whose opinion you trust, and then incorporate any feedback that person gives you into the activity.

## 6

# Presentations with a Punch

**QUESTIONS TO PONDER:**

1. What is your modus operandi: media star or a behind-the-scenes person?
2. Can both types become successful teachers in the ITV environment?
3. How can a person with limited artistic experience (that is, still uses stick people) be successful in the use of visual materials?

## TEACHER AS MEDIA STAR

Some of us bloom in front of a video camera and others try to get done and out of camera range as quickly as possible. In our experience, both types of teachers, as long as they have the right training and know how to implement it, can be effective over ITV. The previous chapters have described how to engage and maintain the students' attention through adequate preparation, appropriate pedagogy, focused content, and interactive strategies. But the scariest part for most teachers is examining their own personal style to see how it works over a broadcast medium. The good news is that most people are able to adapt their way of presenting themselves to make it more engaging for the participants.

The following are a few quick tips on presenting yourself well.

---

**Reminders for Media Stars**

1. Take some deep breaths before you start the cameras. Try to relax.
2. Let your enthusiasm show for the subject, students, and the delivery system.
3. Look into the eye of the camera. Use a smiley face on the camera if necessary.
4. Balance eye contact with all participants.
5. Make sure your words and message are clear.
6. Change the quality of your voice—tone and speed—appropriately and often.
7. Make sure the camera is on you when you are talking (not on a blank board).
8. Stay within the range of the camera.
9. Be theatrical! Work the material!
10. Practice, practice, practice!
11. Get feedback on your mannerisms from friends or peers.
12. Watch yourself on tapes to identify problems.

---

Every one of the above tips is important. Amazingly, even simply looking into the eye of the camera can make a world of difference in the success of the lesson. You can't imagine how irritating it is when a teacher doesn't make eye contact with you. It is common for teachers to look persistently at the distant site monitors instead of the camera.

### Voice Quality

Voice quality is a component of teaching that is almost always overlooked in the traditional classroom. Voices have their own personalities that can either stimulate or bore the students. Most teachers don't listen to their own voices except on telephone messages. Tape record your next class and listen carefully to yourself. Ask yourself the following questions:

✓ Do you purposefully use your voice to emphasize points and make transitions?
✓ Is your voice quality generally pleasing, or is it too shrill or too low to hear?

✓ Do you pronounce words clearly? Could a limited English proficient student understand what you say?

✓ Close your eyes and listen. Does it sound like the person speaking is enjoying what she is doing and wants to share that with others?

## Movement

Another technique that is used by instructors (with different degrees of effectiveness) is to vary motion or movement. A teacher's movement can be used to emphasize a point or illustrate a process; movement to a different camera can signal a switch in topic or the use of an example. Movement of props can simulate reality to clarify a concept—teachers have moved small soldiers over a battlefield to illustrate the relationship between what was planned and what actually occurred, and why. And don't forget that regularly changing the in-use camera will simulate movement for the students who are viewing the screen.

ITV teachers need to be aware of the way they move. Repetitive mannerisms like jingling keys or playing with hair can drive observers crazy over time. At the same time, hands are not only visible, but also magnified. Be careful of how they look. The most common problem with teachers new to the camera is stiffness. This can be relieved to a degree by taking deep breaths and thinking "relax," but practice has the biggest impact. The more you practice, the smoother the transitions and the overall flow of content will go.

## Letting Your Dramatic Side Take Over

Because viewing a monitor is a step removed from being present personally, this medium tends to exaggerate weakness. In other words, if someone is a little boring face-to-face, she will be very boring over the system. Monotones seem to worsen; lack of enthusiasm becomes mind numbing. We are not asking for Lucille Ball or Lawrence Oliver, but . . .

Important Point: Overall, most people need to put a little more pizzazz in their style.

Current research says that if they are trying hard, adults can generally pay attention to one topic for 10 to 15 minutes. Many research conferences are lethal because this mechanism for boredom is built in. As teachers, we can circumvent this outcome by changing something about our instruction every 5 to 10 minutes. This change can be as simple as modifying our voice pitch and speed, switching strategies and activities, or even moving to another topic.

In addition to spicing up lessons with increased dramatics, role playing by teachers and students has been used with great success to explain or enhance varying perspectives. Role playing works especially well for students at the distant sites because it can increase their sense of connectivity through a structured, creative activity that promotes communication and reflection. Students can pretend to be television interviewers or game show hosts. Role playing also makes it safe for students with different views to vent their feelings to each other without repercussions.

### Humor

Should you use humor? The general opinion is that humor can be very helpful in keeping students engaged. No, you do not have to be a stand-up comedian, but humor can highlight a point or wake up the masses.

What if I'm not funny? One of the wonderful things about humor is that people are often humorous just trying to be funny. Do what feels comfortable to you. See what happens when you try different comments, stories, and cartoons. If the students don't laugh, that may be a clue, but remember that one of the greatest uses of humor is the ability to laugh at yourself. And be careful not to say anything that you wouldn't want recorded.

Caution: Be sure that the major thrust of the lesson emphasizes its academic content and meaning.

Although theatrics and humor make lessons more appealing, hold attention longer, and are a necessary element in their own right, be careful that they don't become the main focus.

### Dressing the Part

Even though we are encouraging you to be more theatrical in action, this does not necessarily pertain to apparel. Before you rush for your Dr. Seuss "Cat in the Hat" hat left over from Halloween, you need to consider its color and composition. Generally video system specialists caution against wearing: red, white and black; sharp contrasts or busy patterns; flashy and shiny accessories. After saying that, we'll contradict ourselves to tell you that colorful clothing can look good, and some jewelry is just fine. It depends on such things as

- the color of the background behind you (try to avoid both white and black);
- the quality of the cameras and monitors;
- room lighting; and
- how the colors you're wearing change when projected on the monitor.

Another thing to consider is the color of your complexion. We know that real men don't wear makeup, but—no matter who you are—if your complexion is extremely ruddy you might want to tone it down. Dare we mention lipstick? The "Return of the Living Dead" look should be avoided. In the end, the best advice we can give you is to check yourself out on the monitor when the system is not linked to distant sites.

Caution: Be aware of the appearance of your clothes and accessories over the ITV.

Reflection: Surely one of the most difficult processes in the world is to examine your behavior and appearance in order to improve your instruction. Can you put down your defenses and truly look at your approach? What could make this process easier for you?

### TEACHER AS MEDIA SPECIALIST

Important Point: The two most important "gifts" that you have to make interactive television motivating, engaging, and effective, are 1) attention to "aggressive interaction," which we've been discussing in previous chapters, and 2) the effective use of the multimedia component.

The multimedia component of interactive television is an exciting tool that is underused in most ITV classrooms. This is due in part to the failure of teachers to take advantage of new technologies that can reach students through the media they are most comfortable with, namely video.

> We are working with a few generations of young people who have been raised on TV, and when they see a television screen they just sit back and relax. What this means is that the image on their monitor has to constantly change. As college-level instructors, we have to learn to be as creative as most second grade teachers already are (Professor Dave Harmon, Colorado Mountain College, 1999).

Some traditional classrooms do have multimedia elements, but the majority of teachers fail to make full use of current media resources. Teachers are often unfamiliar with the hardware and software, or feel that they just don't have enough time to include other media. And sometimes, copyright laws limit free usage of commercial materials. Whatever your reason for not using multimedia support, forget it! Multimedia can make or break your presentation.

Glossary: **multimedia**—a combination of sound, print, graphics (drawings and photographs), and motion picture elements that help convey the message.

## Sound

In current ITV practice, the sound element (including audiotapes and the audio portion of film clips, as well as the participants' voices) is seen as a support for the visual component. Even when sound is featured, as in an audio interview of a famous person, for instance, photographs will likely be used to enhance the presentation. The importance of sound might only be recognized when the video equipment is down and there is no picture. (This has been known to happen, so it is a good idea to have a radio-style lesson plan handy as backup).

However, brain research associated with student learning is extolling the benefits of the use of music even by itself. The addition of music has been found to focus attention on important concepts, aid in the memory of content, and create the ready-to-learn ambience for students. All of these elements could be used in the ITV classroom. For example, classes held after lunch could be stimulated to an "awake" state by playing a short clip of swing music to introduce the war (WW II) years.

Appendix A—See list of books on brain research. This movement was born in the worlds of medicine and science, and is now being applied in exciting ways to education.

## Visual Imagery

In interactive television, the use of visual imagery is a double-edged sword. It is easy to integrate visual components into a lesson plan in order to support learning and motivation, but if they are not used effectively the results can be disastrous. It is difficult to wake up from a monotonous video. In fact, if you're an insomniac, try watching one of those particularly boring educational videos for teachers—it will put you to sleep in five minutes.

 Glossary: **visual imagery**—a visual representation of an idea or concept used to support learning.

*What Does Effective Use of the Visual Component Do?*

*Using visual resources:*

➢ Engages the students' interest. You may be a very interesting person, but a short clip of two scorpions fighting will get students' attention quickly while introducing them to a unit on desert animals.

➢ Evokes emotional responses. Photos appeal to everyone. A discussion of the political history of China will touch the students if illustrated with photographs of the students in Tiananmen Square.

➢ Makes complicated ideas easier to understand. Can you imagine trying to put together Barbie's van without a diagram? A short video clip that shows the airflow over an airplane's wing helps students understand how planes fly and how aerodynamics work.

➢ Simulates reality. Students and other fragile human beings cannot go into the center of a volcano to see the action of the lava, but watching a computer simulation can help them get a clearer picture of the processes involved.

➢ Expands area of experiences. Field trips can be made to remote sites over a video camera with the teacher. Students can experience the construction of a skyscraper without the liability problem.

➢ Enlarges items for closer observation. So often it is difficult for the student in the back to have a good look at the petri dish without the danger of dropping it or disturbing the contents. Art pieces can be enlarged to examine brush strokes or other details.

➢ Connects to students' affinity with video-based activities. Our younger generations are much more attuned to video environments. Having a class watch a commercial and evaluate what they truly know about the product and their experiences with marketing can introduce a unit on fact and fiction.

➢ Helps memory and retention. Discussions support a certain degree of retention of materials, but highlighting words, using graphics that show relationships, showing the content in the context of the real world, and so on, helps students remember the information covered. Seeing video sections of the Nixon–Kennedy debate will help retention more than just reading about it. Current brain research also emphasizes the use of music to aid memory.

➤ Adds variety to a lesson. Who wants to listen to the same person all period? Shifting gears frequently maintains the students' attention span. A quickly delivered slide show can provide context for the study of Italian architecture. Using a selection of swing music to introduce the World War II time period will get the students' attention.

## Improving Instruction with Multimedia Tools

Ok, so adding a variety of media selections makes the lesson more interesting and compelling. What tools do I have to work with and how do I use them? First, you need to start thinking visually and concentrate on "showing" versus "telling." Is there a still or moving image that can convey your message more effectively? If not, can you adapt or create an image that would? The following section discusses each tool that can create visual images.

*Text*

Text is usually displayed on the screen through the use of the overhead camera or a character generator with computer software (see chapter 2 for descriptions). Many systems do not have a character generator or computer capabilities as part of their hardware. If you don't have a technician that runs the cameras for you, you probably don't have a character generator.

The overhead camera and the character generator with software are similar in a number of aspects. For example both:

✓ Can show essential points;
✓ Need to use fonts 24 points or larger;
✓ Must use four-by-three aspect ratio (landscape versus portrait);
✓ Can use presentation software such as Power Point;
✓ Can add colors and graphics; and
✓ Can save creations for later use.

But the overhead camera and the character generator are also very different. The overhead camera is used extensively by ITV teachers, not only to show text and photographs, but also physical items such as maps and math manipulatives. The character generator and associated software can split the screen, write over the teacher's face (or below it), and do voice-overs and other magical things not possible without a technician.

---

### What Does It Look Like?

**Use of Text**

Sally teaches a math class over the ITV. Today the class is studying angles. She uses text by

1. showing how the angles fit into an outline of figures in the beginning of the class. She shares the outline over the Elmo at the beginning of the class.
2. labeling each figure she holds and discusses. She sets the model of each angle under the overhead camera and on its printed name.
3. sharing the written definition over the system. The definition slide has been created by Power Point and uses a 24-point font and the landscape format (four by three). The white border around the outside doesn't circle more than five lines of text.
4. creating a study guide that uses the geometric terms and definitions with activities that might include the use of filling in the blank or listing elements.

> Right angle—an angle that measures 90 degrees. Modern day homes have mostly right angles.

---

*Graphics*

Glossary: **graphics**—visual images used to illustrate a point, clarify a meaning, or just decorate the page.

You can create and collect graphics with or without a computer. Without one, teachers can draw their own sketches or borrow drawings from students, peers, and others. Pictures can be cut and pasted from printed materials or even from catalogues that are designed for presentations. These pictures can be combined with text or used by themselves.

If you have a computer you can create graphics with software programs, or cut and paste them from a commercially sold graphic database. In addition, you can copy graphics from paper by using a scanner that can copy the graphic onto a disk. Be aware that graphics use a lot of memory, which can be a problem if you are trying to save them on a floppy disk to transport into the system.

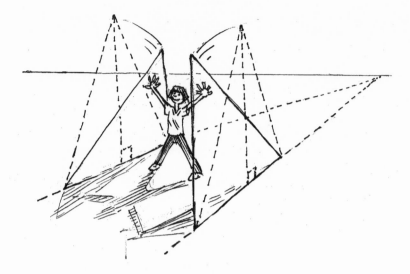

How you display graphics depends on your system. All systems have overhead cameras. Using the overhead camera means that the graphic to be shared is on a "hard copy" and placed on the pad under the camera. On the other hand, you don't need a hard copy if your system has the capacity to use graphics directly from a disk. If you have a technician, your system can probably do this directly from the control panel. (Having a technician means that someone else is controlling the cameras.)

 Glossary: **hard copy**—information printed on paper (versus information on a computer).

If you don't have a technician, you need to check on this capability. Some set-ups do connect a computer with the system to provide a way to use software over the system even without a technician and his control panel.

---

**What Does It Look Like?**

**Use of Graphics**

Sally also uses graphics in her geometry class. She draws the three types of angles under the overhead camera and describes each characteristic of the angle as she draws that component. At each site, the students have manipulatives in the shape of triangles. The students proceed to trace each triangle and measure the sides and angles. To her previous definitions of angles, she adds drawings that illustrate each angle.

## *Photographs or Slides*

Personal photographs or slides created by students, teachers, friends, or commercial photographers can be integrated into your class materials to emphasize a point or describe a concept. With permission from the photographer, teachers can build libraries of photographs or slides that support ideas stressed in class. Mounting frequently used photographs will save work in later years. Photographs and slides can be examined for the overall effect or specific details. They can also be used for their aesthetic appeal when coupled with music to create a mood. There are also commercial libraries of photographs available for use by the public on CDs and through the Web. Again the four-by-three ratio is best for balance, but photographs that are not four-by-three can be used on plain backgrounds.

Because of the enlargement capacity of the camera lens, interactive television provides an especially good medium for looking at small photos. Photographs can be used directly under the overhead camera or scanned for use through a computer or a more sophisticated control panel.

---

**What Does It Look Like?**

**Use of Photographs**

Sally has collected a series of photographs that she shares with her class using the overhead camera. The students take turns picking out all the right angles that they can find. Many of the photographs are humorous with buildings sitting at strange angles.

The students then look at photocopied photographs on their desk and find all the angles that they can in the photo. The students then measure these angles and copy them onto a chart that has columns for each type of angle.

The students' homework assignment is to cut out photographs at home and measure the legs and angles. Their second assignment is to research why their culture uses so many right angles and if there have been cultures that used other type of angles in their architecture.

---

Important Point: When making photo-mosaics, be aware that some colors look completely different on the monitor, and some color contrasts won't work at all.

Caution: Whether using text, graphics, photographs, slides, or objects, do not forget and leave the overhead camera facing down for long periods of time.

## *Video Clips*

As with photographs, video clips can be created by the students and teachers, or taken from films produced professionally. Because of copyright issues, there is more flexibility with video clips designed by teachers and students. History teachers can show footage from trips to Gettysburg or from a battle enactment. Students can record interviews with senior citizens about economics in the past.

Short video clips have been used successfully in introducing topics, stimulating discussions, interviewing experts, showing context, and explaining concepts. Guest speakers who cannot visit the class because of time or distance can be interviewed at their convenience, and with permission, be viewed during class and in future classes.

Because of copyright laws, sections of professional videos need to be used with permission, or be part of a package that allows ITV classroom use. Due to the time-consuming nature of the process, permission should be sought for an extended time period; this will allow you to avoid duplicating the request every year. Request forms should be easily accessible and the process started before the class starts.

 Important Point: Be careful that you only use a focused selection to emphasize a predetermined point: spending the whole class period watching a movie is a waste of airtime. If you would like the students to see the whole selection, assign it as homework and make sure it is available through the class, school, or library.

---

**What Does It Look Like?**

**Use of Video Clips**

Sally believes that using video clips in geometry helps make the subject less dry and more relevant. In her class she has used video clips that

1. interviewed a parent who is an architect;
2. showed the use of angles in buildings from her trip to Spain;
3. explained how to measure a tree by an onsite demonstration led by a group of previous students; and
4. discussed the history of geometry in a cartoon format created by the National Science Foundation.

---

*Chroma-keys System*

This is a familiar technology to anyone who watches the TV weather report. When you see a guy standing in front of the weather map pointing to fronts and systems, he isn't standing in front of a map at all. What is really behind him is a blue screen—a computer adds the map. This is very slick technology that has just become available for ITV systems. If you do get a chance to use it, be aware that if you're wearing clothes the same color of blue as the screen the clothes will disappear. In that case you will become a strange, disembodied assemblage of hands and head. That's a neat effect if it's done intentionally, and if it isn't you'll have a hard time keeping your students focused on what you're trying to say.

Glossary: **chroma-key system**—a technology tool used with a video camera for inserting images behind the presenter.

*Simulations*

Visual imagery plays a role in computer software programs that simulate a world or a process. A lot of literature has been written on the microworlds that computers can create. We are not interested in the purely entertainment worlds, but in using educational software that creates environments to study concepts or theories. Some software programs create worlds in order to see environmental or political impact of adding specific variables. Other software programs simulate science experiments or even the results of cooking using the correct or incorrect measurements. Some very exciting math simulations help clarify ideas that have defied easy explanations. One of the authors never really understood what binary equations were until the older software program "Green Globs" illustrated the process. The purpose of simulations is to emphasize the showing of content/process versus the telling of content/process.

Glossary: **microworld**—a virtual environment that exists on a computer and can be manipulated by the user.

If you don't have a system with a built-in computer in the control panel, and it is not possible to add a computer to the cables, a camera may be able to focus on the computer monitor screen (sometimes the image is fuzzy, so check it out beforehand). Depending on the subject content, having the ability to show computer simulations may be a very useful tool.

---

**What Does It Look Like?**

**Use of Simulations**

Sally has found a software program that manipulates geometric figures while showing real-life uses of geometry. She uses the program sometimes to illustrate a point or introduce a new topic.

---

*In Conclusion*

Using technology that relies heavily on its visual component has forced educators not only to look at what they are presenting, but *how* they are presenting it. The old "teaching by the seat of your pants" method all but eliminates the possibility of fully utilizing the video tools that are available. To take advantage of multimedia possibilities requires time for planning and obtaining the necessary resources. The exciting news is that the more attention you pay to your style of presentation and the multimedia tools, the more interesting your teaching will be not only to your students, but also to you.

## CHAPTER 6 KEY POINTS

1. All teachers can become better instructors by improving their presentation style and incorporating multimedia tools.
2. A number of presentation tips, such as looking at the camera rather than the monitor, help the audience feel like you are interacting with them.
3. The quality of your voice and movement can be used to capture interest and improve understanding, or bore and irritate the students.
4. Generally, most teachers need to relax more and to be more thoughtfully dramatic in their style. Humor also helps to maintain attention.
5. What you wear, from clothes to jewelry, can enhance or distract from the content of your lesson. When in doubt, you should preview items on camera.
6. The use of multimedia components such as sound, text, graphics (drawings and photographs), video clips, and computer simulations makes instruction over ITV more effective.
7. Multimedia components can be used by teachers to engage interest, make complex issues easier to understand, simulate reality, aid memory, and increase variety, among others.
8. Every multimedia tool can be used with all subject content, but time is necessary to plan and obtain resources.

## LIGHTS, CAMERA, ACTION

1. Examine your formatted lesson plan created in chapter 4 and expanded in chapter 5.
2. Review what you had written for the media support column. With the new information from this chapter, refine and enhance that column.
3. Create and collect the resources you will need for the media support, such as drawings, photographs, video clips, computer software, etc.

# 7

# Making Evaluation Work for You

**QUESTIONS TO PONDER:**

1. If it were not required, why would we ever want to spend the time doing an evaluation?
2. How can we learn the most about our class or program without feeling overwhelmed?

## TEACHER AS EVALUATOR

Most teachers are swamped with day-to-day planning and teaching. ITV teachers are swamped with day-to-day planning and teaching and creating and col-

lecting multimedia materials that will
allow them to use the ITV system to its
greatest advantage. So why would
teachers want to spend yet more time on
planning and implementing an evaluation, or gathering, analyzing and reporting data?

 Glossary: **evaluation**—a systematic investigation of the worth
or merit of an object or process.

Experts provide us with many purposes for evaluation. Feedback from our
evaluation can

> ➢ show us our program's growth and impact;
> ➢ provide clues for improving our classes;
> ➢ help us communicate more effectively about our efforts;
> ➢ show our accountability to the community;
> ➢ to justify spending; or
> ➢ to fulfill a requirement (in other words, because we *must*).

However, the main reason given by many teachers and directors for conducting an ongoing evaluation is that most of what they know or do is based on guesswork, and they would like to have a clearer picture of what is really happening.
A well thought out and carefully implemented evaluation is the only way we
know what is going on, and whether or not the program is making any difference.
After all, why are we putting all this effort into a program if we cannot be sure it
is working? In addition, most evaluations provide both small and large surprises
which help our understanding and produce those "Oh, now I get it" feelings.

 Important Point: Evaluation is a crucial tool for determining
progress, impact, and our growth as professionals—use it!

 Reflection: If you performed an evaluation on your current
work, what would be some of the reasons for doing it?

Evaluation is not new to educators. Most administrators and teachers are informally evaluating their programs as they proceed. Student assessment, which is

part of evaluation, has traditionally been tied to all forms of instruction. What do we want to do with evaluation, as teachers or program directors, that is different-from what we normally do?

What we are mostly advocating and hoping to provide is an emphasis on purpose and organization. In our past experiences, we have seen teachers implement activities and teaching models that have failed because they did not have their goals and desired outcomes clearly in mind.

If you are a project director for an ITV system, there is probably a written description of your goals and objectives somewhere. Or, if your responsibilities are mainly focused on classroom teaching, you need to be sure of what skills you want your students to get from their learning experience (chapter 3 discusses alignment with standards), and the best way you can help them acquire those skills. Then you have to be sure that you have an accurate way of measuring progress towards those objectives. Evaluation tools are helpful in measuring progress that culminates in measurable outcomes (the tools are described towards the end of the chapter). This chapter is designed to help you clarify your thinking and provide structures for better organization of your efforts.

 Important Point: The evaluation process is *so* much easier if the pieces are clearly defined before any action takes place; namely, before the program or class begins.

## The Three-Pronged Attack

We have found that, for most educational efforts, looking at evaluation from three directions makes the most sense. *Implementation evaluation* is basically looking at how well the program or class is being implemented. This component includes all the variables that have to do with operational issues discussed in chapter 2, that is, how well the class or program is being conducted. Logs, checklists, or surveys can be designed that reflect those variables. For example, a teacher log could provide data on how many times classes were cancelled due to technology difficulties, or if materials were delivered on time at distant sites.

Important Point: The secret to this type of evaluation is making sure you consider *all* the appropriate variables.

Evaluators sometimes compare the evaluation process to cooking. If you use this analogy, evaluating how well you follow the recipe would be implementation evaluation.

If you don't have guidelines from a grant you are implementing, a good beginning is to get the staff or peers together to create a list of all the implementation factors. Then logs, checklists, or surveys can be designed to evaluate the success of these variables. The end of each year is an appropriate time to review the findings.

Caution: No person or project is perfect. Allow yourself to be open to the results of the evaluation, and use them for improvement.

*Formative evaluation* is part of what teachers do informally on an ongoing basis. How do we constantly improve what we are doing in the classroom or in our program? We are lucky in that interactive television lends itself to this type of feedback because of the video capacity. Videotapes of the classes can be reviewed for personal style issues with the teacher, effectiveness of lessons, attention of the students, depth of the discussion, and student interactivity. The videotapes can show us how we need to improve; other data, such as grades and test results, can alert us to the idea that something needs to be improved.

*Surveys* are also good for providing data that aid improvement, but surveys are often conducted only at the end of a semester, which is too late for contributing to ongoing improvement. You should still use surveys, but you need other input during the semester. Interviews and focus groups can be used to identify information that can improve the classes. Facilitators are an excellent source of ongoing feedback.

Glossary: **focus group**—a small group of carefully selected participants that discusses predetermined questions.

Important Point: The secret to formative evaluation is to pick a time at regular intervals to review the data.

All of us have good intentions to review our data, but before you know it, it is the end of the year and the "reviewing data at regular intervals" has disappeared with other good intentions like reading more professional journal articles and calling friends more often.

> Using the same cooking analogy, formative evaluation would be the tasting of the stew as you make it. This tasting tells you to add more salt or make other improvements.

*Summative evaluation* answers the question, "so what?" Implementation and formative evaluation can tell you how well you conducted your class or program and how to improve it, but summative evaluation asks what impact you or your program have made. Sometimes evaluations go into beautiful descriptions of what the staff did, but never get to the point of what kind of difference it made.

Important Point: If you spend all the time and energy planning and teaching a class, you want to know if it was worth it!

*Summative evaluation* data to examine at the end of the semester (or year) include surveys, grades, interviews, observations, students' work, and other types of students' assessment.

Important Point: Often, the secret to meaningful summative evaluation is to measure impact over time.

Most of us can learn anything for a short period of time, but have your students really integrated the material into their learning in such a way as to be able to refer to it in one or two years? This sounds like a complex longitudinal study, but the process can be as simple as mailing letters with self-addressed postcards to previous students. The questions on the cards can ask if they have applied the learning, and how well they remember what they had learned.

Glossary: **longitudinal study**—research done over an extended time period that focuses on a select group of subjects.

Again returning to the analogy of cooking, summative evaluation would be the guests' reactions to the stew that was prepared. Was it pleasing or was it a waste of time? Maybe they should have gone out for a hamburger!

Reflection: What types of evaluations have you participated in, in the past?

## First Purpose, Then Organization

What is your purpose for doing an evaluation? Before you can start organizing your evaluation you need to have its purpose(s) clearly defined. The section above was included to help you decide what type of evaluation you will do—although your choice might be a combination of types. You may want to look at impact at the end of the year, and also to check in during the year to see how you can improve your class or program. Sometimes deciding *whom* you are doing the evaluation *for* helps determine your purpose(s). Is this evaluation for you, the students, the school board, the dean, or the funding agency?

Caution: Be sure that your evaluation is not just a list of strategies and activities accomplished.

*The Magic Matrix*

| Needs | Goals/Objectives | Strategies/Activities | Outcomes |
|-------|------------------|-----------------------|----------|
| 1.    |                  |                       |          |
| 2.    |                  |                       |          |
| 3.    |                  |                       |          |

We find the above matrix very helpful in organizing the evaluation process. The first column lists the needs. The needs are the impetus for the instruction or program to be implemented. They identify features that have been overlooked or require revision. For an ITV classroom, such needs could include:

➢ lack of student expertise in an area,
➢ lack of peer support for learning,

> ➢ lack of expertise and resources at hand to support instruction, and
> ➢ lack of adequate staff development.

The needs should be supported by documentation. For example, test scores or grades from previous classes can document lack of student expertise. In the case of the other three examples listed above, needs can be documented by the results of a survey.

When the needs are clearly defined, determining the goals and objectives becomes easier. If the students lack sufficient expertise in reading, then the goal must be for them to become better readers. The objectives break the goals down into tasks that are of a manageable size to attack. Being a better reader can mean a number of things, but for our example let us say it means having increased comprehension and vocabulary. See the following figure.

| Needs | Goals/Objectives | Strategies/Activities | Outcomes |
|-------|------------------|-----------------------|----------|
| Students are poor readers (documented by entry exam) | Students will become better readers <br> - comprehension will improve, and <br> - vocabulary will improve | Strategies include: <br> - peer coaching, <br> - time designated for reading, <br> - skill analysis and practice, and <br> - group reading clubs | Students will increase their norm-referenced reading scores by 5 NCEs each year. |

So now that we know what our needs, goals, and objectives are, how do we go about implementing them? That effort is carried out through the strategies and activities. If we are not clear about our goals and objectives, we won't know if our strategies are supporting progress toward them. It is the "If you don't know where you are going, you'll end up somewhere else" syndrome.

The strategies and activities suggested above may help the students become better readers, but we can only find out by testing the students to see that the instruction has yielded outcomes. Outcomes need to be exact. Initial questions in the definition process include: what student group will be targeted by the instruction, to what degree the outcomes will be achieved, and when the outcomes will be measured. In the example above, the participating students will take a norm-referenced test that will show a growth of five NCEs each year.

Glossary: **norm-referenced tests** (NRTs)—commercially produced tests that use a selection of items to determine how a test taker's ability compares to that of a larger group, usually the district, the state, and the nation.

Glossary: **criterion-referenced tests** (CRTs)—tests that focus on the comprehensive examination of a specific area of academic content; end of the chapter, end of the level, end of the semester, and end of the year tests are usually criterion-based tests.

Important Point: Even if you aren't performing an evaluation, the Magic Matrix is an excellent tool for organizing your program or class. Use it!

Outcomes can be measured by a large assortment of tools, including tests, checklists, surveys, observations, attendance records, and notes from meetings. The more concrete the outcomes, the easier it is to determine if they have been achieved. The earlier example of the 5 NCEs is good, because it is easy to determine mathematically whether or not the outcome has been achieved.

Glossary: **normal curve equivalents** (NCEs)—a score that is comparable to percentiles, but has equal value between each interval of one. For example, the difference between 97 and 98 NCEs is the same value as between 49 and 50. NCEs are handy because you can average themore easily.

Reflection: What are the specific desired outcomes of the course or program that you are currently working on?

## Data Collection

So how do you know if you have achieved your proposed outcomes? You gather data. Sounds simple, doesn't it? Gathering data is about as simple as determining your outcomes. Both tasks seem to be fairly easy processes at first glance, similar to perhaps making crepes (flour, eggs, milk, and baking powder). How difficult can it be with so few ingredients? We won't even go there.

Important Point: The secret to creating good, measurable outcomes and an easy data collection process is scheduling plenty of time up front for the reflection process.

Just as the outcomes must be specific, and address the core issue of why you are putting in all of this hard work to begin with, the data collection process must be well-defined and focused before you start. What types of data will address your outcomes and what are the best means of gathering them? Sometimes educators gather too much data, at other times not enough. An example of this "overgathering" and "underutilizing" is found at almost any school, where there are file cabinets full of old tests and nothing significant done with the information they contain.

Reflection: In your classroom, do you make full use of the information that can be found in performance assessments and test results? If not, think of new ways to use them.

On the other hand, because of lack of data, many teachers work in the dark about such things as whether that new math approach is making any significant difference. Or, even if they know that the approach does make a difference, they may not know what components make the approach successful.

Important Point: The best data to work with are concrete.

Handling data is easier when they are in numerical form. Test scores, grades, attendance, passing rates, and graduation rates are already in numerical form (1, 2, 3, 4, and so on). Other sources of data, such as surveys, observations, performance assessments, and journals, require extra steps to organize into quantitative form. This process will be discussed more thoroughly in the sections that describe specific tools.

## Tools that Help

Data can be gathered from records, colleagues or peers, students, and even your own experience! Data can be quantitative, with nice rows of numbers, or qualitative, with descriptive pieces that add interest to dull numbers. The following tools have been used with distance education programs and classes.

### Tools You Can Use by Yourself

Journaling and completing a self-assessment are good places to begin in evaluating both yourself and the course or program.

Glossary: **journaling**—writing in a journal at regular intervals and reflecting on the writing.

Journaling has been popular for hundreds of years, but has experienced a surge in popularity among educators in the last decade. What is amazing is that, while teachers encourage students to write regularly in journals to improve their writing or anchor math concepts, few teachers actually write regularly in their journals to improve their teaching! (The key word here is regularly.)

Why should teachers spend time writing every day in a journal? Because *you* are the best source of data and thinking when it comes to evaluating your class or program. And regretfully, details don't stay with us from day to day. (In fact, some of us have noticed serious loss of detail the older we get.)

Journaling is approached in a number of ways.

- Some teachers write everything they can remember from that day.
- Some teachers write around themes or questions.
- Some teachers write to the objectives from the evaluation.
- Some teachers write down as much as they can remember, then go over the text to see if any patterns are noticeable.

 There are some great articles on journaling, including *The Swamp Log* by Frank Nicassio. This article provides a structured, in-depth approach to journaling (*SwampLog: A Structured Journal for Reflection-in-Action*, Frank Nicassio, 1992).

Journaling can provide information on progress, insight into patterns, and rich scenarios for reports. There have also been cases where teachers worked out personal problems in journals, but that is another book.

Self-assessment has been popular with ITV teachers, as it is a tool that helps put some objectivity into the self-reflection process. In addition, using a comprehensive assessment helps target elements that may have been forgotten. The wonderful, comprehensive self-assessment in Appendix B is based on the key points from this book, and has been designed to help you reflect on your planning and instruction. To complete the form, you can fill in the answers from memory, or better yet, use videotapes from either practice lessons or previous lessons as a source for your answers.

 Other sources of good self-assessments include Virtual Classroom and Teleclass Teaching (*Virtual Classroom: Educational Opportunity Through Two-Way Interactive Television*, Hobbs and Christianson, 1997; and *Teleclass Teaching: A Resource Guide*, Cyrs and Smith, 1990).

As all evaluation involves some degree of reflection, journaling and self-assessment forms are effective tools. However, since they are "self-reported," the findings would be more valid if they were combined with data from other sources.

*Tools You Can Use with Your Peers*

Colleagues or peers can be valuable resources in providing feedback. Minimally, you can ask them to watch one of your classes (or taped video) and give you input on how well the class went. Even better would be for your colleagues to watch a class and fill out the appropriate elements of the self-assessment form. If they also teach an ITV class, you can return the favor by giving them input on their classes.

The whole concept of "critical collegiality" appears at times to be a delicate dance. Peers can be wonderful sources of data—who would understand teaching and students better than another teacher! But giving input to another teacher can be fraught with danger. Remember, you *do* have to teach with this person.

Caution: Be careful with your verbal input!

Some helpful hints on working with your colleagues include:

- ✓ Be compassionately critical, not recklessly ruinous. Fellow ITV teachers need feedback on how to improve their instruction. Telling them of distracting mannerisms will help them improve their instruction. Telling them they look like idiots when they utilize those mannerisms will not improve their instruction or your relationship.
- ✓ Be honest and appropriate. You should point out where they are speaking in a monotone. Pointing out that this characteristic matches their personality is not appropriate.
- ✓ Be clear in your own mind that your opinion is from your perspective and that you are not God. (Actually the sense of control in running an ITV classroom can lead to feelings of omnipotence . . . until the equipment fails.)
- ✓ Give concrete examples to support your opinion. Vague comments are not helpful. "You talk funny" doesn't lend itself to effective improvement. "You tend to rush your words when nervous" is more helpful.

Reflection: Do you have a hard time being honest with colleagues, even when they ask you for feedback? How can you give yourself permission to do this?

Another tool found to be very helpful is an observation form that looks at time the students spend on task. This type of tool was created to indicate how engaged the students are in their lesson. Hopefully, if the lesson is going well everyone in the class will be paying attention. To use this form, you will need a friendly colleague to observe the students at each site. You don't want your cohort trying to observe more than five or six students at a time. The total class period is divided into 5-minute intervals.

**Observation Form**

Class _____ N = nonverbal attention

Date _____ V = verbal attention

Observer _____ D = distracted

| TIME | STUDENTS | | | | |
|------|---|---|---|---|---|
|      | 1 | 2 | 3 | 4 | 5 |
| 8:30 |   |   |   |   |   |
| 8:35 |   |   |   |   |   |
| 8:40 |   |   |   |   |   |
| 8:45 |   |   |   |   |   |
| 8:50 |   |   |   |   |   |
| 8:55 |   |   |   |   |   |
| 9:00 |   |   |   |   |   |
| 0:05 |   |   |   |   |   |
| 9:10 |   |   |   |   |   |

Every five minutes, the observer glances around the room at the targeted students to see how involved they are with the presentation or activity. Then the observer notes their engagement with a code letter in the form. The codes can vary, depending on what you want to know. As noted on the form, the sample uses: nonverbal attention (N), verbal attention (V), and distracted (D).

Important Point: Each observer needs to physically be at each site to observe the targeted students.

Observing the students' actions isn't as easy as observing the teacher's actions, because the teacher, as one individual, tends to have a lot of camera time. Every observer will need to be able to see each targeted student at his or her site clearly. Seeing each student consistently is not possible from another site because, if you followed him with the camera, the student and everyone else would know when you were watching him.

After looking at the results, if many of the students were not paying attention during the class, it is time to rethink what you are doing.

*Tools You Can Use with Others*

This category includes many types of tools, including tests, surveys, performance assessments, checklists, interviews, focus groups, and written documentation. When we talk about tests, we are assuming a tool with a numerical score associated with it. This distinction needs to be made because some performance assessments have types of percentile scores, while others may have rubrics (a type of scoring over a short range of numbers), and some do not lend themselves to numerical scoring. So tests with numerical scoring would include teacher-made tests, CRTs, NRTs, and performance assessments with scores.

Glossary: **performance assessment**—an assessment that demonstrates the process of thinking and its outcome, not just the memorization of isolated bits of knowledge.

Directions for administering and scoring accompany most tests. They can be scored by hand or by the publisher (test company). The publisher can tabulate the scores for you in a specific form upon request. Be sure you have the scores in a format you can manipulate and disaggregate.

Caution: Test scores appear to be straightforward, but can be misleading if they are not disaggregated.

Glossary: **disaggregation**—breaking test scores down to learn more about subgroups.

Disaggregating takes time and reflection. Think of what you would like to know and reorganize the numbers to help you get a clearer picture.

Appendix A contains a list of books about evaluation. These are "user friendly" books that can help beginners and experts.

Performance assessments that can be used as tools for ITV evaluation/ assessment purposes include: student journals, student products, student presentations, and portfolios. Sometimes these terms overlap; for example, a student product might be found in a portfolio.

The ITV system lends itself to the use of student presentations. Student presentations make a good cumulating activity at the end of a unit. A student presentation can demonstrate how well the student understands the concepts. This application of the learning builds the self-concept of the presenter and gives the other students a chance to ask questions and offer suggestions for improvement.

---

The general biology class has just finished a unit on the classification of plants. For a final project, the students were asked to select 5 plants from different species. The students were to introduce the plants by discussing their predominant characteristics and how they are classified.

The students made their presentations over the ITV. They had samples of the actual plants, but also brought in photographs and drawings. Some of the students even made short video clips of the plants' environments (where they picked them). Chris, one of the more entertaining students, caused a lot of laughter and interest by formally introducing the plants as though they were debutantes at a ball. Students had a chance to question the presenters at the end of their talks.

---

Surveys are a favorite tool of evaluators for a number of reasons. By using surveys you can gather information from a large group in less time than by interviewing everyone. Surveys can be standardized, so you can use them repeatedly for different classes and different years. In addition, the surveys can be formatted to evoke numerical answers, thus cutting down on time spent in tabulating the results. On the negative side, surveys almost always take longer to design, administer, and tabulate than you think, and the information is self-reported (which mean the respondents could lie or even be mistaken in their perceptions).

In the ITV classroom surveys can be used:

- to see if there is interest in the student body in taking an ITV class;
- at the beginning and/or end of a class or year with the participating students to examine process and impact;
- with your peers concerning their perceptions of the classes, program or technology; and
- even with parents or the community to see how they perceive your efforts.

Surveys can be used to get feedback on any aspect of your instruction or program. An elementary math program used the following survey to examine younger students' perceptions of the ITV classroom. The surveys were designed to be anonymous.

When creating your own surveys, be sure that each question asks exactly what you want, clearly and without confusion. In addition, the responses need to fit the

## Two-Way Interactive Television: Student Survey

Class_____Site_____

Please check your response to the following statements:

SA = strongly agree   A = agree   U   = undecided   D = disagree   SD = strongly disagree

|  | SA | A | U | D | SD |
|---|---|---|---|---|---|
| 1. I can easily see the TV monitors from where I sit. | | | | | |
| 2. I can easily hear the teacher from where I sit. | | | | | |
| 3. The teacher can hear me when I ask questions. | | | | | |
| 4. I have enough space to do my work. | | | | | |
| 5. The teacher pays the same amount of attention to all the sites. | | | | | |
| 6. Most of the talking and asking of questions is done by the students in the room with the teacher. | | | | | |
| 7. I get to know students from other schools. | | | | | |
| 8. I would like to meet students from other schools more often in person. | | | | | |
| 9. Student behavior is better in the ITV classes than regular classes. | | | | | |
| 10. Often the ITV class is boring. | | | | | |
| 11. I would rather take an ITV class rather than a regular class. | | | | | |
| 12. My parents like the idea that I am taking an ITV class. | | | | | |

answer. Be sure to try each question with each of the possible responses. Also, ask yourself, "will you know anything new after you get the responses back?"

Caution: Always ask a peer to take the survey before the first time you administer it, and have him give you feedback on content and clarity.

Checklists are often neglected and misunderstood. Using a checklist to help record progress or determine impact seems too easy to be an "official" evaluation tool. But in reality, checklists can help organize meaningful data. Let's give check-lists a chance! What data can you collect that would lend itself to a checklist?

Typically, ITV teachers do not use formalized interviews or focus groups as sources of data for the evaluation of their classes or programs. However, there might be a time in their evaluation process when these tools would be useful. Interviews would be a good choice if the data you need is known by one or just a select number of people, and the information is such that it can't be explored sufficiently in a survey. The interview questions would be structured, but open-ended. Whoever does the interviewing should be trained, or at least have read some information on effective interviewing techniques.

A focus group is a different animal. This strategy would include a small group of people who come together to brainstorm or discuss an issue, a question, or a problem. Again the questions are formed ahead of time and a facilitator and a recorder (or a tape machine) are needed. Focus groups are helpful when you need the synergy of a group.

Another rich source of data is found in written documentation. This documen-tation could include: administrator notes, teacher evaluations, attendance logs, meeting minutes, newspaper articles, and student folders. Using written docu-mentation is usually time-efficient as it is already prepared for analyzing. A num-ber of teachers know what type of data they will need and so collect the written documentation during the year in files that they can use later.

Reflection: Which of the discussed tools could you adapt for your own use?

## Analyzing the Data and Reporting

After all the data are collected, you organize them by grouping and "ungrouping" (disaggregating) elements.

Qualitative data can be transformed into numerical form or used for anecdotes in reports. Survey or interview answers that are open-ended can be organized into numerical categories. Checklists can be tabulated, thus creating numbers. Test scores are already in numerical form.

Glossary: **qualitative data**—descriptive data, or data that are in a non-numerical form like remarks, insights or observations.

Data that have a large number of variables, like tests or surveys, can be entered into a database to be number crunched (statistically maneuvered). Many of the statistical procedures need specific alignments of data, so be careful. If determining things like standard deviations sends you into a tailspin, think about cross tabulating instead. Cross tabulating is just matching variables, and can be done fairly easily with the appropriate software.

 Glossary: **cross tabulating**—sorting two or more variables to determine and display linkages. However, you need to know what variables to combine and how to use the program.

 Caution: Don't try doing the difficult statistical functions yourself, unless you've had specific training or have a professional evaluator as a friend or employee.

The goal in this entire process of looking at all the data is to simplify and to see the relationships between variables. For example, after you have tabulated the survey and disaggregated the test scores, is there an agreement on what instructional component appears to be working in perception from the survey and reality from the test scores? The more the different data sources agree on an insight or conclusion, the stronger the case. After some effort, these insights and conclusions will be linked with the outcomes.

Methods of reporting your results include:

- a summary using transparencies (or presentation software) to the school board or the dean of the college;
- a report to the community through a newspaper article;
- a written report to your funding agency; or
- a discussion of the findings with other teaching staff over coffee.

A good format for presenting evaluation results includes background on the program, how you conducted the evaluation, and presentation of the main conclusions along with supporting data.

 Important Point: The people you report to will want the report to be easily understood and interesting. Know your audience. Don't be enamoured of too much detail.

## TEACHER AS RESEARCHER

### Action Research

Another way of measuring impact is called "action research." Teacher as observer and researcher is at the core of this philosophy. Teachers record observations

from their classes and reflect on what approach or strategy could improve the instruction or class management. These ideas can then be discussed with peers and researched in the literature. Or the teachers as a group can discuss how to address specific challenges and decide on an approach supported by research. The teacher or teachers then try the approach or strategy and record observations about the results. The group then discusses the results and the "action" is amended or continued or discarded.

The school board had asked the high school principal about the effectiveness of the high school distance learning program. Some of the board members felt that learning over a television could not be as successful as having a teacher in the classroom. They wanted some proof that the classes were worth the district's financial investment.

The high school principal went to the distance learning teachers and told them the situation, and asked if they could collect some information that would show the progress and impact of their program. The three teachers met together and decided that the purpose of their examination or evaluation was to show the school board whether or not their classes were effective.

They decided to address two objectives that focused on subject content, skills learned, and overall growth in language arts (speaking, listening, reading, and writing). For a comparison group, they decided to use data from the same subject classes, using only those classes that were given before the advent of the ITV classes. The data that the teachers gathered included current and past: grades, the state performance tests scores, semester tests, attendance, student presentations, student surveys, video clips, and interviews.

After fairly extensive data collection and synthesizing, the teachers summarized their findings: Although the content and skills that were acquired in the ITV classes were similar to those in the traditional classes, a vast improvement was seen in the students' language arts skills such as speaking and listening, and in some cases, reading and writing. Their conclusion was that the pedagogy used in the ITV classes required students to use a variety of language arts skills in order to have high levels of interaction. The students were doing more assigned reading, writing, and presenting than in a traditional classroom.

Action research can be implemented in a more formal manner with supervision by an outside entity, or more informally with a group of peers. The scenario on page 115 provides an example of one teacher's approach.

Reflection: Do you think some of your colleagues would like to consider doing some action research? What topic would be of the highest priority?

Jim writes in his journal every day after school. He notes that he has mentioned many times throughout the first month that the fifth period class does not seem to focus on the materials as well as the other classes. He perused videos of previous classes to see if his perceptions were correct. The class did seem to be less involved, but it was difficult to be sure. He then asked colleagues to observe the fifth period class at the different sites and record involvement on an observation sheet (see Tools that Help, page 105). The sheets confirmed that many of the students were not engaged throughout the lesson, but it was one specific site that seemed to have the lowest involvement.

At the next meeting of the ITV teachers, he asked his friends/peers (including the colleagues that had observed the classes) what their best thinking was on why there was this lack of engagement. After a brainstorming session, a number of ideas were suggested.

One of the topics discussed was that this particular site was composed of students just beginning at their institution and that not only were they relatively new to the school, but new to ITV instruction, and relatively young in years compared to the other classes. Some suggestions included gearing examples and illustrations to a younger group or having more interactive hands-on activities.

Jim began using more age-appropriate illustrations, integrated more interactive strategies which used cooperative learning, and even led a discussion with the fifth period students on change and being in a new environment and what made it easier or more difficult.

He continued his observations/journaling and a month later asked his colleagues to observe the class. He and his colleagues agreed that there had been an improvement in engagement. However, he was not sure if it was due to the new activities or just the addition of more attention to the class.

## In Conclusion

This chapter was intended to help you design and conduct your own evaluation. You aren't expected to use every strategy or tool discussed. On the other hand, most of the topics discussed have entire books written about them and we had limited space. If you want more information, the articles and books in the resource list can be found at bookstores, libraries, or on the Internet.

Helpful hints on the overall evaluation process:

- Keep the whole process as simple and focused as possible (unless you have big bucks for a professional evaluator).
- Identify and prioritize the objectives that are most important. You may not have time for all of the components.
- Be absolutely clear up front about what you want to know and exactly how you will get that information.
- Consider what data you already have.
- Look for examples of the tools. You may not need to recreate them.
- If possible, don't do the evaluation by yourself. It is more fun and easier with a colleague.

## CHAPTER 7 KEY POINTS

1. The reasons to conduct an evaluation are varied and include showing growth and impact to help improve the class or program, to aid communication, to prove accountability, to justify spending, to meet a requirement, and to take the guesswork out of educational decision making.
2. Having the purpose and organization firmly established in the beginning makes the evaluation process easier and more valid.
3. Three types of evaluation to consider are implementation, formative and summative evaluation. Implementation evaluation looks at how well the evaluation is being conducted, ongoing formative evaluation gathers information that can improve the program, and summative evaluation measures impact.
4. Scheduling regular meetings after designated time intervals helps keep the feedback loop intact.
5. Measuring impact over time can be useful for judging instructional approaches.
6. The need for a class or program should define the objectives. The objectives should be carried out through the use of strategies and activities. The result of this process would be the measurable outcomes.
7. Sources of data include journals, self-assessments, observations, tests, surveys, performance assessments, checklists, interviews, focus groups, and written documentation.
8. After the data are gathered, they need to be arranged in a form easy to analyze. Most data need to be tabulated and synthesized, numerical data needs to be disaggregated, and qualitative data needs to be categorized or used for anecdotes.
9. The goal of analyzing data is to more clearly see patterns and the relationship of the variables to the outcomes.
10. Regardless of the type of evaluation report, it should be easy to understand, to the point, and as interesting as possible.
11. Action research not only uses support teachers as researchers, but helps improve programs, supports staff development, and decreases feelings of isolation.
12. Hints on doing an evaluation include: keep it simple, prioritize efforts, be clear up front, use what has already been done, and don't do it by yourself.

## LIGHTS, CAMERA, ACTION

1. Think about a class or program you are teaching or implementing. Using the Magic Matrix form from this chapter, determine the needs, objectives, strategies/activities, and outcomes of your class or program.

2. Make a list of tools and methods that you could use to gather data to show progress toward the outcomes.
3. To whom could you present a report on this evaluation and why would you want to?

*8*

# That's What It's All About: Chapter Summaries

This final chapter of *Shifting Focus* is a summary of its contents, chapter by chapter. We decided to end the book this way for three reasons:

1. you might have a short-term memory problem;
2. summaries are great for quick reference;
3. you might be standing in a bookstore, trying to choose between *Shifting Focus* and *Mein Kampf*—this chapter will help you make up your mind.

## CHAPTER 1: SETTING THE STAGE

*Shifting Focus* is designed to help you deal with the basic technology of two-way interactive television *before* you have to use it. But technology is only one of the issues you'll be facing as you switch from the traditional to the ITV classroom. Just as important is the move into a learner-centered rather than a lecture-centered pedagogy. Because lecture-oriented teaching creates mind-numbing boredom when broadcast over ITV, you will have to change or adapt your pedagogy to focus on constant interaction with and among your students.

Distance learning ranges from correspondence-based courses to telecommunications-based courses. Full-motion, two-way interactive television is the next best thing to being there. Other video-based technologies offer lesser degrees of interaction. Although this book is specifically directed to a teacher working in the two-way interactive television environment, it is also "backward compatible" with other video-based delivery systems.

At its best, ITV takes advantage of the diversity that occurs when a classroom is made up of students from different sites and backgrounds; it enhances student interaction rather than reducing it, and greatly expands limited course offerings. At its worst ITV is a terrible mismatch between technology and education, reducing relationships among teachers and students to sterile interactions.

New instructional paradigms create an instant need for teacher training, but most ITV teachers begin with no experience on the system and little or no training. The effectiveness of ITV technology depends on teacher training, expertise, and willingness to play and make a few mistakes. *Shifting Focus* is intended to be a practical guide to teaching over ITV. It is designed so that as you make your way through it, you will also be creating interesting, thought-provoking, and interactive ITV lessons.

## CHAPTER 2: TAKING CARE OF OPERATIONAL ISSUES

Because, in most cases, ITV teachers work closely with support personnel, it is very important for you to be a team player. The most common members of the team are the teacher, site facilitators, and equipment technicians. The only way to keep the team working smoothly is to have regular meetings over the system, which can easily be scheduled before or after the transmission of the class.

Facilitators range in training and expertise from certified teachers to parent volunteers. Site facilitators are an integral part of the ITV classroom. Most facilitators make sure the equipment is on and running, distribute materials, assignments, and assessments, and (to varying degrees) monitor discipline and assist in instructional activities. No matter how busy you get, it is crucial to maintain good relationships with your facilitators and other team members.

Even when everything runs smoothly, teaching over an ITV system is a challenge. Activities such as setting schedules, planning lessons, and creating standards of discipline should all happen before classes begin. Scheduling a number of schools to share an ITV class is extremely complicated, and should be handled the year before the class begins. Remember that your ITV class is a production, and should be planned as such. Make sure that all members of the team have had introductory training on the equipment.

It is important to consider not only the smooth administration of the program, but what to do if the normal procedure is interrupted. Plan ahead for such unforeseen events as absent teachers and facilitators, or nonfunctioning equipment. Because the equipment is intimidating to most newcomers, be sure that all members of the team have had time to familiarize themselves with the classroom and everything in it before the class begins.

There is a large variation among ITV classroom set-ups, ranging from the bare minimum to ready-for-commercial-broadcasting. Both ends of the spectrum have advantages and disadvantages for the ITV teacher. Equipment found in most ITV classrooms includes monitors, graphic cameras, character generators, microphones, fax machines, VCRs, and computers. With all this equipment, it is inevitable that one component or another will go down. There are logical plans that can be carried out in case of equipment malfunction.

There are a number of operational strategies that provide learner support at a distance. A procedure must be in place to answer students' questions either in class or after class by e-mail or telephone. Turnaround time should also be short for assignments and tests—comments have more impact when they are immediate and personalized. Some of the basic ITV classroom equipment will support you and the rest of the team in responding quickly to your students.

There are also a number of outside resources that can support ITV instruction. These include libraries, other schools, and community centers. Any of these may have links to the Internet, and can be utilized to enhance instruction and learner support.


## CHAPTER 3: WHAT TO TEACH AND HOW TO TEACH IT

Because ITV pedagogy rests on a high degree of interactivity between the teacher and students, traditional learning models may not work. Even teachers whose learning models incorporate interactivity may have to redefine their roles from presenters of information to facilitators of the learning process. Fortunately, there are a few models that you can rely on to help you make the switch.

Our own experience, supported by research, indicates a strong link between effective instruction over ITV and the constructivist theory. According to this model, learning becomes a process of knowledge building that engages both the teacher and the students. To implement it, you have to make your instruction experiential and relevant, and give the students a chance to interact with the materials in such a way that they will construct their own representation of the learning objectives.

As questions are often the basis for interactivity, using the pedagogy of inquiry-based instruction will also help you become an effective ITV teacher. With this approach, both students and teachers become data gatherers and analysts without undermining the teacher's role as facilitator. As in the constructivist model, the teacher facilitates a process of investigation and analysis rather than delivering a prefabricated body of knowledge. Using the inquiry approach you can create a structure, based on a leading question and a set of subquestions, which will encourage your students to create their own focus and pursue their own inquiries. In the process they will analyze information they have collected and team with you and their classmates to arrive at conclusions.

Not only do both of these learning models encourage interactivity, but they also reinforce critical thinking skills and create a link between academic knowledge and the ability to understand and analyze what is happening in the world outside of the classroom.

Good ITV instruction is developed out of cooperation and teaming when students are interactive and involved. But it also depends on aligning the content of the teaching materials with standards that have been developed for your grade level and/or subject area. It is possible to use fun and innovative themes and strategies within the context of defined standards, but it takes teacher/staff time and effort. First, it is necessary to familiarize yourself with the content and performance standards.

## CHAPTER 4: GETTING READY

The only way to create a successful lesson over ITV is to prepare in advance. But for most teachers, planning for ITV classes takes more time than planning for the traditional classroom. This is partly because teaching over interactive television involves more dimensions than in the traditional classroom, and partly because the camera magnifies mistakes, dead time, awkward mannerisms, and so on.

The success of your instruction depends on meeting the needs of your students, and the best way to do that is to get to know them. There are several tools that will help you to tailor your lessons to the needs of your students, including questionnaires, surveys, and personal inventories (but ideally, these need to be sent out before the class begins). The multiple intelligence model can also help align instruction to the various learning styles in your classroom.

Once you understand the needs of your students you can begin writing the actual lesson plans. Although it is possible to get along without formal lesson plans in a traditional classroom, a written plan is crucial to your ITV instruction. One way of creating a well thought out, chronological lesson plan is to use a simple two-column format with the lesson outline in the first column and the accompanying media support in the second.

The two-column lesson plan can be distributed to the rest of the team, so that the facilitators and technician will be prepared for their own roles. If possible, a practice run should be timed to guarantee that the lesson does not run beyond the allotted time. Because equipment failure is always a possibility, the entire team needs to be prepared with copies of a back-up lesson that can be taught independently at each site.

Because teachers typically borrow ideas and materials from other sources for the sake of good instruction, copyright is something that has to be taken into account, even in the traditional classroom. But because ITV is a broadcast medium, copyright is a more serious issue. To make matters worse, copyright laws in the relatively new realm of educational technology are often poorly defined and open to misinterpretation.

There are "fair use" provisions of copyright laws that apply specifically to educational situations, which means that in some cases you can legally borrow material for presentations over ITV. Because this is such a complicated issue, it is best to use suggested resources to familiarize yourself with copyright issues. But the bottom line is that it never hurts to seek permission, and when permission is granted, to give copyright credit on written copies or in the credits of films, videotapes, etc.

## CHAPTER 5: SO FAR AND YET SO NEAR

One of the greatest challenges you will face as an ITV teacher is to reduce the students' perception of physical separation. When you have students at "remote" sites connected to your classroom by nothing more than electronic magic, you have to create a cohesive, interrelated group. There are five categories of strategies that promote interaction: those that develop interpersonal relationships, use questioning activities, use real-life people and places, use drama to create interaction, and emphasize cooperative learning. Most these are familiar to you from your work in traditional classrooms. All of them focus on decreasing distance by creating dynamic, cooperative relationships among the players in your ITV classroom.

You can create a learning environment that promotes genuine human contact by being a human being, yourself. Let the students know who you are and create situations that will encourage them to get to know each other. Spend one or two class sessions on introductions and helping the students become accustomed to being on camera.

In the ITV environment the only way to fight the talking head syndrome is to keep the students interacting with you and each other. One of the best ways to do this is to foster an atmosphere in which questions can (and do) flow in any direction. In addition to using the inquiry approach, it is important to be prepared with other questions pertinent to the day's material. When asking questions, keep careful track of turns and pay equal attention to your students at the remote sites.

Active learning gives students a sense of ownership of their own learning process. ITV students are more willing to invest effort in the learning process when the learning materials are relevant and meaningful—focusing learning materials on real-life situations goes a long way toward ensuring that they will be both. A good way to promote active learning (and satisfy the "relevancy criterion") is to engineer learning experiences that occur outside the scope of class materials, or to bring local activities into the ITV classroom. Fieldtrips and interviews (both virtual and real time) can perform these functions.

All students learn better when they feel responsible for their learning and actively participate in the process. Because motivation is so important in the distance learning environment, this is even more crucial in the ITV classroom. In addition, we have found that discipline isn't a problem when the students are engaged. Participatory activities, like group problem solving and student presentations, promote engaged learning and are easy to incorporate into the ITV classroom.

The sense of connectedness that happens with interaction is the single most vital element in the ITV classroom. There are several interactive teaching strategies that encourage all three types of interaction. These include role-playing activities, simulations, and interactive games. Encouraging collaborative work is an essential part of interactive teaching; building relationships should be a specific and constant focus of an ITV teacher. Collaborative activities include group problem solving, peer teaching, debates, and brainstorming.

## CHAPTER 6: PRESENTATIONS WITH A PUNCH

Whether you are a performer or a shrinking violet, you can adapt your way of presenting yourself on camera to become more engaging over the broadcast system. There are several tips that will help you do this—some of them seem self-evident but still require practice. Looking into the eye of the camera, for instance, can make a world of difference to students who get irritated by teachers who seem to be staring into space as they speak.

Voices have personality and can either stimulate or bore the students. Teachers rarely hear themselves speak, so record your next class and listen to your voice. Realize that your voice is a great tool for capturing interest and creating emphasis. Practice using this tool until you do it well. Your own body movements can be used in the same way. Movement can emphasize a point or illustrate a process; it can signal a change of pace or topic, and movement of props can simulate reality to clarify a concept.

Let your dramatic persona take over, but be aware that the camera will also exaggerate weaknesses. Be careful about your clothing and makeup—check yourself out on the monitor to see if everything works over the system. Repetitive mannerisms can be really annoying, a monotonous voice will send everyone off to sleep, and stiffness will make you look like a mannequin. Generally, most teachers need to relax and be more thoughtfully dramatic in their style. The more you practice, the better your presentation will be.

Humor tends to bring people together. You don't have to be a stand-up comedian, but making your students laugh will keep them engaged and help them remember important points and concepts. Even though we're encouraging theatricality, you don't want to make your students laugh at the wrong thing (your clothing, for example). Generally, video system specialists caution against wearing red, white, and black; sharp contrasts or busy patterns; and flashy or shining accessories. You should check your appearance on the screen when the system isn't linked to distant sites.

Multimedia backup for instruction has exciting potential that is minimally exploited in most ITV classrooms. Multimedia components can be used to engage interest, make complex issues easier to understand, simulate reality, aid memory, and enhance a variety of teaching strategies. Every multimedia component, including sound, still photographs, movie and video clips, and graphics, can be used with any subject content, but time is necessary to plan, create, or obtain resources.

## CHAPTER 7: MAKING EVALUATION WORK FOR YOU

Even though ITV teachers may be swamped with other chores, performing ongoing evaluations helps measure the growth and impact (or lack thereof) of your programs and classes. Feedback from evaluations can also provide clues for improving your classes, help you communicate better about your efforts, provide accountability, justify how you spend money, or sometimes just fulfill a requirement. All too often in education, the bottom line is that much of what we know and do is based on guesswork; evaluations give us a clearer picture of what is really going on and whether or not it is making any difference.

The evaluation process can be complicated, so it is important to have the specific purpose of your evaluation, as well as its organizational structure, firmly established in the beginning. There are three main categories of evaluation: implementation evaluations look at how well the program is being conducted; ongoing formative evaluations gather information to be used for program improvement; and summative evaluations measure the impact of the program. Some evaluations focus on only one of these categories, while others include all of them.

The first step in organizing an evaluation is to determine why the class or program is taking place; to do this you have to identify the need(s) for it. Once the needs are established, you can define the objectives that will be accomplished in order to meet the needs. Predefined strategies and activities, also defined during the organizational process, set out the steps for reaching the objectives. The result of this process is measurable outcomes, and the job of the evaluation is not only to measure them, but to analyze progress made toward meeting the objectives.

Sources of data include journals, self-assessments, observations, tests, surveys, performance assessments, checklists, interviews, focus groups, and written documentation. Once these data are gathered they must be arranged to facilitate the process of analysis; most data need to be tabulated and synthesized. Quantitative data need to be disaggregated, and qualitative data need to be categorized or used for anecdotes. The goal of the data analysis is to uncover or clarify patterns and relationships among the statistical variables and the measurable outcomes.

There are many ways to report the results of your evaluation—some of them formal (for example, a formal report submitted to the funding agency) and some informal (for example, a presentation given to the school or institution staff). Regardless of the type of report, it should be to the point, easy to understand, and interesting.

Another way of measuring impact is to do action research. This puts you, the teacher, into the role of observer and researcher, and it contributes to program improvement and staff development. Whatever type of evaluation you are conducting, keep it simple, prioritize your efforts, be up front, don't duplicate someone else's efforts, and don't do it by yourself.

*Appendix A*

# Further Reading

## BRAIN RESEARCH/MULTIPLE INTELLIGENCES

*Brainstorming and lightning bolts: Thinking skills for the 21st century*
David D. Thornburg
David D. Thornburg and Starsong Publications
1998

*Making connections: Teaching and the human brain*
Renate Nummela Caine and Geoffrey Caine
Association for Supervision and Curriculum Development
1991

*The unschooled mind: How children think and how school should teach*
Howard Gardner
Basic Books Inc.
1991

## CONSTRUCTIVIST/INQUIRY

*Handbook of research in education, communication, and technology*
M. Duffy and D. J. Cunningham
Macmillan
1997

*Learning through geography*
Frances Slater
Heinemann Educational Books
1982

*Visual tools for constructing knowledge*
David Hyerle
ASCD ID: 196072S25
April 1999

## COPYRIGHT

*The copyright primer for librarians and educators*
J. H. Bruwelheide
American Library Association
1995

*Multimedia and learning: A technology leadership network special report*
J. H. Bruwelheide
National School Boards Association
1994

## DISTANCE EDUCATION

*Distance education: Strategies and tools*
Barry Willis, Editor
Educational Technology Publications
1994

*Linking for learning: A new course for education*
Office of Technology Assessment
Congress of the United States
1989

*Teleclass teaching: A resource guide*
Thomas E. Cyrs and Frank A. Smith
New Mexico State University
1990

*Virtual classrooms: Educational opportunity through two-way interactive television*
Vicki M. Hobbs and J. Scott Christianson
Technomic Publishing Co., Inc.
1997

# EVALUATION

*At your fingertips*
Karen Levesque, Denise Bradby, Kristi Rossi, and Peter Teitelbaum
MPR Associates
1998

*User friendly handbook for project evaluation: Science, mathematics, engineering, and technology education*
Joy Frechtling, Editor
National Science Foundation
1996

*Disaggregation* (web site)
http.//www.remc8.k12mi.us/bridges/disag.html

# INTERNET

*Educator's Internet companion: Classroom Connect's complete guide to educational resources on the Internet*
Gregory Giagnocavo and Tim McClain
Prentice Hall Computer Books
July 1996
ISBN: 0-13-569484-1

*Internet directory for teachers,* 1st Edition
Grace Jasmine and Julia Jasmine
IDG Books Worldwide
December 1997
ISBN: 0-76-450219-0

*The Internet for teachers (for dummies),* 2nd Edition
Bard Williams
IDG Books Worldwide
November 1996
ISBN: 0-76-450058-9

*Internet kids and family yellow pages,* 2nd Edition
Jean Armour Polly
Osbourne/McGraw-Hill
June 1997
ISBN: 0-07-882340-4

*New kids on the net: A tutorial for teachers, parents and students*
Sheryl Burgstahler
Allyn & Bacon
February 1997
ISBN: 0-20-519872-4

*Science on the Internet: A resource for K-12 teachers*
Jazlin V. Ebenezer and Eddy Lau
Prentice Hall
October 1998
ISBN: 0-13-095918-9

*World Wide Web for teachers: An interactive guide*
Ralph Cafolla, Dan Kauffman, and Richard Knee
Allyn & Bacon
October 1996
ISBN: 0-20-519814-7

## MULTIMEDIA/TECHNOLOGY

*Mac multimedia for teachers*
Michelle Robinette
IDG Books Worldwide
November 1995
ISBN: 1-56-884603-7

*Multimedia in the classroom*
Palmer W. Agnew, Anne S. Kellerman, and Jeanine M. Meyer
Allyn & Bacon
January 1996
ISBN: 0-20-516408-0

*Using technology in the classroom*
Gary G. Bitter and Melissa Pierson
Allyn & Bacon
January 1999
ISBN: 0-20-528769-7

# *Appendix B*

# Teacher Self-Assessment

| Characteristic | Application<br>1 = never<br>2 = occasionally<br>3 = frequently<br>4 = often<br>NA = not applicable |
|---|---|
| **Chapter 1** | |
| 1. I make a conscientious effort to establish rapport with my students. | 1  2  3  4  NA |
| 2. I avoid doing most of the talking or being a "talking head." | 1  2  3  4  NA |
| 3. I make as many opportunities as possible for student participation. | 1  2  3  4  NA |
| 4. I continue to read, watch, or listen to ways of improving my ITV teaching. | 1  2  3  4  NA |
| 5. I visit other ITV classrooms to get ideas and support. | 1  2  3  4  NA |
| 6. I use a journal or a similar tool to reflect on my teaching and classroom dynamics. | 1  2  3  4  NA |
| **Chapter 2** | |
| 7. I have a good working relationship with my ITV team members. | 1  2  3  4  NA |
| 8. The site facilitators/technicians are clear about their roles and responsibilities. | 1  2  3  4  NA |
| 9. I have regular scheduled planning time. | 1  2  3  4  NA |

| Characteristic (continued) | Application |
|---|---|
| 10. I have regular scheduled planning time with the facilitators/ technicians face-to-face or over the ITV. | 1 2 3 4 NA |
| 11. I encourage members of the ITV staff to offer suggestions and ideas. | 1 2 3 4 NA |
| 12. I provide outlines, lesson plans, and other materials to the facilitators and technicians in plenty of time for them to prepare. | 1 2 3 4 NA |
| 13. I share ideas with other ITV teachers in the building at conferences or electronically. | 1 2 3 4 NA |
| 14. I know how to operate the ITV equipment and feel comfortable about doing it. | 1 2 3 4 NA |
| 15. Everyone connected with the ITV program has had some training on the equipment. | 1 2 3 4 NA |
| 16. The scheduling for my classes is completed a good deal in advance of the start of classes. | 1 2 3 4 NA |
| 17. I am aware of time zone differences if there are any. | 1 2 3 4 NA |
| 18. I review rules and student contracts with the students at the beginning of the course. | 1 2 3 4 NA |
| 19. I have an adequate budget for materials and copyright approvals. | 1 2 3 4 NA |
| 20. I have identified ITV-trained substitutes in case I am absent. | 1 2 3 4 NA |
| 21. I have lesson plans prepared that can be used in case of equipment failure or other emergencies. | 1 2 3 4 NA |
| 22. I have created a handbook that lists ITV procedures, settings, and key phone numbers. | 1 2 3 4 NA |
| 23. I am familiar with "panning" and "zooming" and know when to apply these features. | 1 2 3 4 NA |
| 24. I know how to work with the four-by-three ratio of the camera's projected image. | 1 2 3 4 NA |
| 25. I know if my set-up has a character generator and how to take advantage of its abilities. | 1 2 3 4 NA |
| 26. I know where the microphones are located and have provided guidelines for the students on their use. | 1 2 3 4 NA |
| 27. I have access to a FAX machine and know how to use it to deliver immediate communications. | 1 2 3 4 NA |

| Characteristic (continued) | Application | | | | |
|---|---|---|---|---|---|
| 28. I know how to encourage student motivation and interest by using the VCR for private and commercial video clips. | 1 | 2 | 3 | 4 | NA |
| 29. I know if my system has a CD-ROM and where to find discs that are applicable to my class. | 1 | 2 | 3 | 4 | NA |
| 30. With help from a technician, I have created a trouble-shooting list for my ITV system. | 1 | 2 | 3 | 4 | NA |
| 31. I help students arrange study groups. | 1 | 2 | 3 | 4 | NA |
| 32. I respond to questions and test papers as quickly as possible. When possible, I make individual notations to the students. | 1 | 2 | 3 | 4 | NA |
| 33. I make sure materials are delivered on time to students at distant sites. | 1 | 2 | 3 | 4 | NA |
| 34. I use the Internet to support student learning. | 1 | 2 | 3 | 4 | NA |
| **Chapter 3** | | | | | |
| 35. I have students find information, rather than giving it to them. | 1 | 2 | 3 | 4 | NA |
| 36. I do more facilitating than directing. | 1 | 2 | 3 | 4 | NA |
| 37. I use a variety of tools to assess students. | 1 | 2 | 3 | 4 | NA |
| 38. I link learning to real-life situations. | 1 | 2 | 3 | 4 | NA |
| 39. I help students see ideas from many perspectives. | 1 | 2 | 3 | 4 | NA |
| 40. I provide experiences that help students work collaboratively. | 1 | 2 | 3 | 4 | NA |
| 41. I provide experiences for the students to draw their own conclusions. | 1 | 2 | 3 | 4 | NA |
| 42. I encourage my students to be data gatherers and analysts. | 1 | 2 | 3 | 4 | NA |
| 43. I use the distance between sites to enhance the quality of data gathered. | 1 | 2 | 3 | 4 | NA |
| 44. I am committed to all my students achieving the standards or comparable measures. | 1 | 2 | 3 | 4 | NA |
| 45. In my planning, I reflect on both stated and hidden beliefs that will be taught. | 1 | 2 | 3 | 4 | NA |
| 46. I reach out to the community for support and to share our efforts and results. | 1 | 2 | 3 | 4 | NA |

| Characteristic (continued) | Application |
|---|---|
| **Chapter 4** | |
| 47. I have a good grasp of my students' knowledge and experiences. | 1  2  3  4  NA |
| 48. I know what my students' needs are in the subject area addressed by my instruction. | 1  2  3  4  NA |
| 49. I adapt my lessons to match different learning styles. | 1  2  3  4  NA |
| 50. My lesson plans with media components are completed in advance of the ITV classes. | 1  2  3  4  NA |
| 51. I use a variety of media tools and materials to enhance my instruction. | 1  2  3  4  NA |
| 52. My class never goes over the allotted time period on the ITV system. | 1  2  3  4  NA |
| 53. I get permission if I am in doubt about a copyright issue. | 1  2  3  4  NA |
| 54. My program or building has established copyright guidelines for our specific needs. | 1  2  3  4  NA |
| **Chapter 5** | |
| 55. I incorporate strategies that improve interaction by improving interpersonal relationships. | 1  2  3  4  NA |
| 56. I incorporate strategies that use questioning activities to improve interaction and learning. | 1  2  3  4  NA |
| 57. I incorporate strategies that use real-life people and places to engage the students in interactive learning. | 1  2  3  4  NA |
| 58. I incorporate strategies that use drama to create interaction. | 1  2  3  4  NA |
| 59. I incorporate strategies that emphasize the use of collaborative groups to encourage interaction. | 1  2  3  4  NA |
| 60. I share who I am with the students. | 1  2  3  4  NA |
| 61. I call on my students by name. | 1  2  3  4  NA |
| 62. I use humor during my class. | 1  2  3  4  NA |
| 63. I change the pace of the class on a regular basis. | 1  2  3  4  NA |
| 64. I balance my attention between sites. | 1  2  3  4  NA |
| 65. I am aware of the duration and type of questioning I use in the ITV classroom. | 1  2  3  4  NA |

| Characteristic (continued) | Application |
|---|---|
| 66. I use culturally relevant content when possible. | 1  2  3  4  NA |
| 67. I encourage students' presentations for the sharing of findings and as an assessment procedure. | 1  2  3  4  NA |
| 68. I have identified any simulations or interactive games that would support the objectives of my class. | 1  2  3  4  NA |
| **Chapter 6** | |
| 69. I look directly into the camera to make eye contact with the students at the distant sites. | 1  2  3  4  NA |
| 70. I am aware of where the camera is pointing. | 1  2  3  4  NA |
| 71. I check videotapes of my presentations to see if I have any mannerisms or habits that are distracting. | 1  2  3  4  NA |
| 73. I use movement to emphasize points. | 1  2  3  4  NA |
| 74. I experiment with putting more drama into my presentation. | 1  2  3  4  NA |
| 75. I run a trial test on my clothes and jewelry before classes begin to be sure that they are not distracting to the viewer. | 1  2  3  4  NA |
| 76. I avoid using small fonts and too much verbiage with overheads and the character generator. | 1  2  3  4  NA |
| 77. I use my library of graphics, pictures, photographs, and video clips. | 1  2  3  4  NA |
| **Chapter 7** | |
| 78. I have a clear idea what is working and what is not working in my class. | 1  2  3  4  NA |
| 79. I know what my objectives are and how I will reach them. | 1  2  3  4  NA |
| 80. My desired outcomes are clear and measurable. | 1  2  3  4  NA |
| 81. I use evaluation to improve my program. | 1  2  3  4  NA |
| 82. I use evaluation to determine if my program is making any difference. | 1  2  3  4  NA |
| 83. I examine and analyze my data on a regular basis. | 1  2  3  4  NA |
| 86. I share data and findings with colleagues. | 1  2  3  4  NA |
| 87. I disaggregate any test scores. | 1  2  3  4  NA |
| 88. I make sure the right audience hears about the results of my evaluation. | 1  2  3  4  NA |

| Characteristic (continued) | Application |
|---|---|
| 89. I improve my instruction by using action research. | 1  2  3  4  NA |
| 90. I enjoy teaching over the ITV system. | 1  2  3  4  NA |

# Glossary

**bubble survey**—a survey in which responses are marked in small circles that can be read and tabulated by a scanner and computer.

**character generator**—a special computer that generates short messages and displays them on top of the image on the monitor.

**chroma-key system**—a technology tool used with a video camera for inserting images behind the presenter.

**closed question**—a question having a fixed answer.

**constructivist theory**—the idea that learning involves a student's direct interaction with the subject matter, and that understanding comes out of that interaction. The teacher is a facilitator of this process.

**copyright**—exclusive rights to the ownership and distribution of a particular literary, musical, artistic, or dramatic work for a specified amount of time. Copyright doesn't protect a work from being used by others; it just protects it from being copied in its entirety.

**criterion-referenced tests** (CRTs)—tests that focus on the comprehensive examination of a specific area of academic content; end of the chapter, end of the level, end of the semester, and end of the year tests are usually criterion-referenced tests.

**cross tabulating**—sorting two or more variables to determine and display linkages.

**dead time**—intervals when nothing is happening.

**disaggregation**—breaking test scores down to learn more about subgroups.

**electronic fieldtrip**—a virtual fieldtrip made available to students either through a satellite downlink or online using a computer.

**e-mail**—electronic mail. Messages sent and received via a computer and telephone lines.

**evaluation**—systematic investigation of the worth or merit of an object or process.

**fair use**—provisions of copyright laws that allow people to use limited selections of copyrighted works.

**focus group**—a small group of carefully selected participants that discusses predetermined questions.

**four-by-three ratio**—the formula that describes the relationship between the height and width of a graphic designed for display on a TV monitor; we are accustomed to pages that are taller than they are wide (portrait mode)—a camera sees and projects in a "landscape" mode, which is wider than it is tall.

**graphics**—visual images used to illustrate a point, clarify a meaning or just decorate the page.

**hard copy**—information in printed form (versus information on a computer).

**ITV**—two-way Interactive TeleVision—a video communications system that allows simultaneous, two-way audio and video connections across two or more sites.

**journaling**—writing in a journal at regular intervals and reflecting on the writing.

**longitudinal study**—research done over an extended time period that focuses on a select group of subjects.

**list serv**—a list of e-mail users who can send messages to all other members on the same list simultaneously.

**microworld**—a virtual environment that exists on a computer and can be manipulated by the user.

**multimedia**—combination of sound, print, graphics (drawings and photographs), and motion picture elements that help convey the message.

**norm-referenced tests** (NRTs)—commercially produced tests that use a selection of items to determine how a test taker's ability compares to that of a larger group, usually the district, the state, and the nation.

**normal curve equivalent** (NCE)—a score that is comparable to percentiles, but has equal value between each interval of one. For example, the difference between 97 and 98 NCEs is the same value as between 49 and 50. NCEs are handy because you can average them more easily.

**open question**—a question with a speculative answer that encourages the student to reflect and investigate beyond the information given.

**panning**—moving the camera lens right or left across the room.

**performance assessment**—an assessment that demonstrates the process of thinking and its outcome, not just the memorization of isolated bits of knowledge.

**qualitative data**—descriptive data or data that are in a non-numerical form, such as remarks, insights, or observations.

**reflection**—reflection is the process of looking at our actions, decisions, or products, analyzing them by focusing on what we did or are doing, and learning lessons that can be applied to new situations.

**scan mode**—periodic rotation of images on the monitor, from one site to another.

**simulation**—the modeling of a real life process (physical or social) with variables that can be explored and changed, using either a computer model or an interactive process among the students.

**site facilitators**—teachers, paraprofessionals, parents or other adults that facilitate the action at the remote ITV sites.

**split mode**—division of the monitor into quadrants, one for each site.

**technician**—the individual who runs the ITV system (if the job is not being done by the teacher).

**tilting**—moving the camera up or down.

**visual imagery**—a visual representation of an idea or concept used to support learning.

**zooming**—movement of the camera lens forward or backward, causing the item that is being viewed to appear larger or smaller.

# References

Cyrs, T. E., and Smith, F. A. (1990). *Teleclass teaching: A resource guide.* Las Cruces, NM: Center for Educational Development, College of Human & Community Services.

Filipezak, B. (1996). *Putting the learning into distance learning.* [Online], Available: <http://www.lucent.com/cedl/training1/html>.

Gardner, H. (1983). *Frames of mind.* New York: Basic Tools Inc.

Harmon, D. (personal communication, June 1999.)

Hobbs, V., and Christianson, J. S. (1997). *Virtual classrooms: Educational opportunity through two-way interactive television.* Lancaster, PA: Technomic Publishing Co. Inc.

Hutchings-Reed, M. (1994). The copyright primer. In Barry Willis, (Ed). *Distance education strategies and tools.* Englewood Cliffs, NJ: Educational Technology Publications.

Jones, B. F., Valedez, G., Nowakowski, J., and Rasmussen, C. (1995). *Plugging in: Choosing and using educational technology.* Oak Brook, IL: Council for Educational Development and Research, North Central Regional Educational Laboratory.

Kemp, J., & Smellie, D. (1997). Planning, producing, and using instructional technologies. In V. Hobbs and J. S. Christianson, (Eds.), *Virtual classrooms: Educational opportunity through two-way interactive television.* Lancaster, PA: Technomic Publishing Co. Inc.

Millbank, G. (1996). Writing multimedia training with integrated simulation. In L. Sherry, (Ed.), Issues in distance learning. *International Journal of Distance Education,* 1 (4), 337–65.

Morris, R. (1986). A normative intervention to equalize participation in task-oriented groups. In E. G. Cohen, (Ed.), *Designing groupwork: Strategies for the heterogeneous classroom.* New York: Teachers College Press.

Nicassio, F. (1992). SwampLog: A structured journal for reflection-in-action, *The Writing Notebook,* 9 (3).

Sherry, L. (1996). Issues in distance learning. *International Journal of Distance Education,* 1 (4), 337–65.

Slater, F. (1982*). Learning through geography.* London: Heinemann Educational Books.

Willis, B., (Ed.) (1994). *Distance education strategies and tools*. Englewood Cliffs, NJ: Educational Technology Publications.

Zehm, S. J., and Kottler, J. A. (1993). *On being a teacher: The human dimension*. Thousand Oaks, CA: Corwin Press, Inc.

# Index

absences: student, 28; teacher, 21, 32, 33, 120
action research, 113, 116, 126
activities. *See* Lights, Camera, Action
"aggressive" interaction, 64–78
assessment: deliver by FAX, 27; performance based, 37, 38, 105, 109, 110, 116, 125; responsibilities for, 17, 120; self, 105, 106, 107, 116, 125, 131–136; state, 44; student, 98, 101
Atlantic Ocean, 49
audio board, 24
audio transmission, 27
authentic instruction. *See* instruction

Belize, 72
Borneo, 73, 74
brain research, 88, 90
brainstorming, 18, 42, 48, 50, 78, 81, 124
budgets, 18, 20

camera: overhead (Elmo, graphic or document), 25–26, 28, 32; room, 33; video, 1, 22–24, 28, 32, 52, 54
caution icons, 5, 11, 16, 17, 19, 23, 24, 25, 27, 28, 29, 37, 41, 44, 55, 57, 67, 71, 73, 79, 86, 87, 93, 100, 102, 107, 109, 111, 113
CD-ROM, 28
character generator, 24, 26, 90–91
China, 89
chroma-keys system, 94–95

classroom: observation, 20, 52, 69, 104–105, 107–109, 114–16, 125; traditional, 3, 7–8, 12, 35, 37,40–42, 52, 62, 64, 72, 75, 77, 84, 88, 94, 122–23; virtual, 9, 95, 106
clothing/accessories, 87
collaborative groups, 76–77
Colorado, 43
Colorado Mountain College, 26, 88
comfortability scale, 13
communication, 1, 9, 45, 86, 116
communities, 40, 41, 47, 71, 72
complex thinking. *See* thinking, higher level
constructivist learning. *See* learning, constructivist
constructivist theory, 37–40, 42, 46, 48
content. *See* curriculum
control room, 24
cooperative learning. *See* learning, cooperative
copyright, 20, 28, 58–61, 88, 93–94, 122–23
course. *See* curriculum
criterion-referenced, 104
critical thinking. *See* thinking, higher level
cross tabulating, 113–115
culture, 53, 71–72
curriculum: biology, 10, 11; computer science, 74; debate, 77, 81; design, 2, 16, 27, 41–42, 72,73; drama, 65; economics, 76; geography 41, 48–49,

# About the Authors

Dianna Lawyer-Brook and Vicki McVey have been friends and associates for more years than they like to count. Their professional collaboration began in Chiapas, Mexico, where they and their children shared a house, an Apple IIc computer, and dissertation woes. Since that first international experience they have written curricula, delivered keynotes, trained personnel, and conducted project evaluations in the United States and abroad. Educational technology and bilingual education have been a focus of their not-for-profit organization and of their personal concerns. One of their favorite interactive television projects involved linking students in rural Kansas and Paris, France, for a world geography class. They are currently helping design a program that uses ITV to deliver instructional content in Spanish to remote rural schools. In addition to their collaborative work, Dianna is part of a statewide team in Colorado that is creating opportunities in technology for college students who want to be teachers. Vicki writes, designs, and edits books.